Cagliostro, The King of the Dead

Books by
Philip J Riley

CLASSIC HORROR FILMS
Frankenstein, the original 1931 shooting script
Bride of Frankenstein, the original 1935 shooting script
Son of Frankenstein, the original 1939 shooting script
Ghost of Frankenstein, the original 1942 shooting script
Frankenstein Meets the Wolfman, the original 1943 shooting script
House of Frankenstein, the original 1944 shooting script
The Mummy, the original 1932 shooting script
The Mummy's Curse the original 1944 shooting script (as Editor in Chief)
The Wolfman, the original 1941 shooting script
Dracula, the original 1931 shooting script
House of Dracula, the original 1945 shooting script

CLASSIC COMEDY FILMS
Abbott & Costello Meet Frankenstein, the original 1948 shooting script

CLASSIC SCIENCE FICTION
This Island Earth, the original 1955 shooting script
The Creature from the Black Lagoon, the original 1953 shooting script (editor-in-chief)

THE ACKERMAN ARCHIVES SERIES - LOST FILMS
The Reconstruction of London After Midnight, the original 1927 shooting script
The Reconstruction of A Blind Bargain, the original 1922 shooting script
The Reconstruction of The Hunchback of Notre Dame, the original 1923 shooting script

CLASSIC SILENT FILMS
The Reconstruction of The Phantom of the Opera, the original 1925 shooting script

FILMONSTER SERIES - LOST SCRIPTS
James Whale's Dracula's Daughter, 1934
Cagliostro, The King of the Dead, 1932

AS EDITOR
Countess Dracula by Carroll Borland
My Hollywood, when both of us were young by Patsy Ruth Miller
Mr. Technicolor - Herbert Kalmus
Famous Monster of Filmland #2 by Forrest J Ackerman

FILM DOCUMENTARIES
A Thousand Faces - as contributor (Photoplay Productions)
Universal Horrors - as contributor (Photoplay Productions)

Mr. Riley has also contributed to 12 film related books by various authors
as well as numerous magazine articles and received the Count Dracula Society Award
and was inducted into Universal's Horror Hall of Fame

CAGLIOSTRO

OR

THE KING OF THE DEAD

An Alternate History for Classic Film Monsters

by

Philip J. Riley

Hollywood Publishing Archives

Published by:
BearManor Media
P O Box 71426
Albany, GA 31708
Phone: 760-709-9696
Fax: 814-690-1559
books@benohmart.com

©2010 Philip J Riley
For Copyright purposes
Philip J Riley is the author in the form of this book

Boris Karloff name and likeness are trademarks of Karloff Enterprises
Script by Nina Wilcox Putnam
John Balderston's treatments by permission by John L Balderston III

Cover Art - ©2010 By Philip J Riley - Since none of the scripts in this series
were thought to exist and were never produced, we have created mock-up posters in the
vintage style of the period.
All photographs are from the Author's collection unless noted

References to the character of The Nubian are in the context of the original 1932 script only. They are not the words of the publisher or author

The Author would like to thank the following individuals who contributed and helped make this series possible.
Carl Laemmle Jr., R.C.Sherriff, Stanley Bergerman, Gloria Holden, Jane Wyatt, Otto Kruger, Marcel Delgado, Robert Florey, Paul Ivano (Cinematographer), Paul Malvern (producer), Elsa Lanchester, Merion C Cooper, Patric Leroux, Bette Davis, Bela G. Lugosi, Sara Karloff, Technicolor Corporation, John Balderston III, Douglas Norwine, Loeb and Loeb Attorneys, David Stanley Horsley, John Teehan
Author's Note: I interviewed the producers, directors, stars, cast and crew in the early to late 1970s. They were recalling events that happened 35-45 years previous and sometimes memory fades or events are recalled from their perspective point of view.

First Edition
10 9 8 7 6 5 4 3 2 1

ISBN: 1-59393-476-9

The purpose of this series is the preservation of the art of writing for the screen. Rare books have long been a source of enjoyment and an investment for the serious collector, and even in limited editions there are thousands printed. Scripts, however, numbered only 50 at the most. In the history of American Literature, the screenwriter was being lost in time. It is my hope that my efforts bring about a renewed history and preservation of a great American Literary form, The Screenplay, by preserving them for study by future generations.
Recommended reading: *The Last Alchemist - Count Cagliostro, Master of Magic in the Age or Reason* by Iain McCalman, Harper Collins, 2003; *The Masonic Magician; The Life and Death of Count Cagliostro and his Egyptian Rite* by Philippa Faulks and Robert L.D. Cooper, Watkins, 2008; *Cagliostro: Savant or scoundrel ? - The true role of this splendid, tragic figure* by W.R.H. Trowbridge, 1910

Cagliostro is dedicated to

Stan Winston

Cagliostro works with Alchemy for a French Nobleman

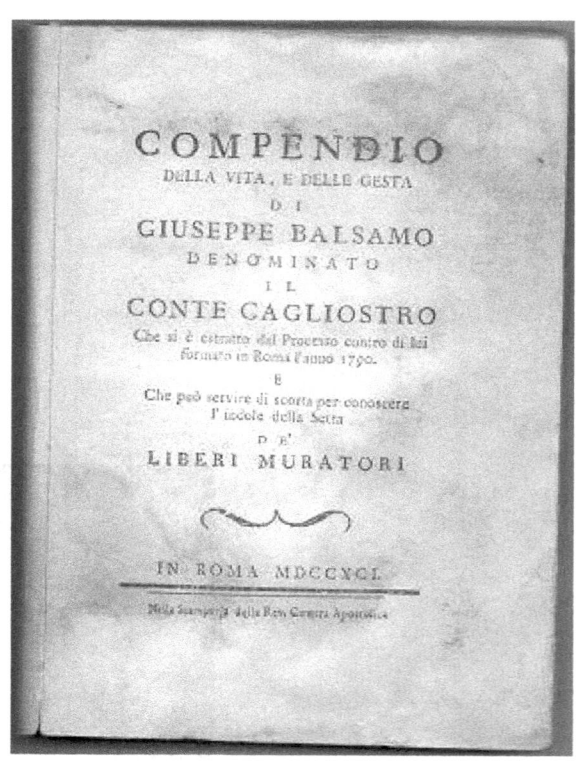

Diary of the Catholic Church's trial of Cagliostro for heresy of being a Freemason; which resulted in his imprisonment where he died.

An old woodcut showing Cagliostro in the court of Marie Antoinette during the "Affair of the Necklace" The extravagance of the necklace contributed to the cause of the French Revolution and almost landed Cagliostro in a cell. - (Getty Archives)

Count Alessandro di Cagliostro

He is considered today, depending on the source, as a charlatan and fraud or as a talented magician, alchemist, physician and pharmacist. His great uncle was named Giuseppe Cagliostro after whom he was named and eventually he added that surname to his imaginary titles.

The man, on whom Nina Wilcox Putnam based her character for her film treatment, was born Giuseppe Balsamo either on June 2 or 8th 1743 to a poor family in Palermo Sicily.

After the death of his father the young Balsamo was uncontrollable and after running away from home a few times he was sent to live with his Uncle. His Grandfather and Uncle tried to assure him a good education but again he ran away and was finally sent to a Benedictine monastery, where he realized he had a talent for chemistry and medicine.

Even the strict discipline of the Benedictines was not enough to control him and he slipped out of the monastery and began an involvement with a local band of gypsies. His gypsy friends gave him his first insights to the occult and alchemy.

He travelled to Egypt, Greece, Persia, India and Ethiopia in the company of an Eastern adept named Althotas. The five years he spent with the adept, visiting mystic temples in Egypt gave him a deeper knowledge of the occult as well as the ability to speak several Eastern languages.

Upon his return to Italy, it didn't take him long to con a goldsmith, named Marano, into giving him a large sum of gold. Before Marano had a chance to see him change a large pile of lead into gold, two thugs, hired by Balsamo, attacked him, rendering him unconscious. When Marano awoke the next day he went to Balsamo's home and found that he had left the country.

From knowledge obtained from the monks of the Catholic Order of St. John, he quickly advanced even more in chemistry and also a series of secret spiritual rites, which he would eventually use to his advantage. For two years he became an auxiliary for the Sovereign Military Order of Malta.

Capitalizing on this position he claimed to be the son of royalty brought up by the Grand Master of the Knights of the Island of Malta.

Now officially Count Allesandro Di Cagliostro, he left the island of Malta and travelled to Naples where he quickly teamed up with the bandits who had previously helped him con the gold from Marano. They plotted to open a casino to cheat wealthy foreigners out of their money. Neapolitan authorities quickly discovered the plan and forced them to leave the city.

In 1768 he moved to Rome, where he not only married a girl named Lorenza Feliciani, but established himself as a doctor. Not long after he became the secretary to Cardinal Orsini giving him Papal access. Becoming quickly bored with this position, he started selling magical, amulets and forgeries on the side. Despite his con games, his reputation grew and he was even recommended as physician to Benjamin Franklyn during his stay in France.

In 1776, he and his wife took and apartment in London, where he spent most of his time in his laboratory. It only took two years before the hangers-on and false friends cheated him out of a large sum of money.

He became a Freemason in 1777 and soon he founded an Egyptian Rite of Masonry which included women for the first time.

Many screen versions of Cagliostro were produced. The first was "The Mirror of Cagliostro 1899 by George Méliès to The Affair of the Necklace starring Christopher Walken in 2001

His next tour was to Germany and it's provinces. At a meeting of Freemasons in Mittau in the Duchy of Courland in 1779 he was asked by the nobles to give an exhibition of his occult powers. Having at first refused the request saying that his powers were not to be used for gratification of the curious, he was eventually persuaded and as a result his followers began to call him a supernatural being.

Cagliostro again settled in Paris in 1785 and his house became notorious almost overnight. Along with Catholic church carvings and prayers on the wall, the main entrance included statuettes of Isis, Anubis and Apis. The walls were covered with hieroglyphics and he and his servants dressed in Egyptian robes.

In 1789 while he was back in Rome trying to establish his Egyptian Rite Temple, he took two men into his confidence. They turned out to be spies of the Inquisition and he was arrested and thrown into a dungeon on the charge of being a Freemason. He died, supposedly, around March of 1795 and his jailer's were confounded by the fact that he had disappeared from his cell thus spreading the rumor that Cagliostro was still alive and 3,000 years old as he had always claimed.

Nina Wilcox Putnam

*A group of prominent writers join together at a banquet to form the Authors' Legion, a branch of the National Recovery Administration. Standing, left to right, are Nunnally Johnston, Rob Wagner, John Russell, Lewis Browns, Horatio Winslow, chairman Rupert Hughes, Jack L. Warner, Jack L. Warner, Jr., W.R. Burnett, Edgar Rice Burroughs; Mark Lee Luther, and Frank Craven. Seated, left to right, are **Nina Wilcox Putnam, author of Cagliostro & The Mummy**, Vina Delmar, Upton Sinclair, and Preston Sturges. (Courtesy John Springer)*

Nina Wilcox Putnam was the author of twelve novels and more than 500 short stories, some of which served as the plots for motion pictures. In her autobiography "Laughing Through" published in 1930, she wrote:

"I was found in a rosebush at the back of Grandma Wilcox's garden at 46 York Square, New Haven Conn., on November 28, 1884."

She was the daughter of Marrion Wilcox, an assistant instructor of English at Yale and an editor of the Encyclopedia Americana. Her mother was Eleanor Sanchez Wilcox from Puerto Rico. The future author, who had absorbed the contents of the family library in lieu of more extensive formal education, worked as an index maker and manuscript reader for G.P. Putnam and Sons. It was there that she met Robert Faulkner Putnam to whom she was married in 1907. Although Mrs. Putnam was married four times she was usually known by the name of her first husband.

She was a flamboyant figure is the pre-World War I Greenwich Village, one of the crowd that frequented the old Brevoort cafe. She sang rollicking songs of her own composition and accompanied herself on a guitar.

Before the War, Mrs. Putnam startled the country by appearing in public in an all-embracing one-piece toga-like garment. She said that she was "protesting against the madness of clothing," and that she had adopted the outfit to rid herself of the fashion designers and fad of style of the day.

In 1911 she sold her first short story for $75, and during World War I followed it up with stories about a hectic character named Marie La Tour.

(From True Origin of the 1040 Income Tax Form?)
by
Michael Jittlov, http://www.wizworld.com

Most folks seem to believe that U.S. citizens have been paying a mandatory tithe ever since the Income Tax was written into the Constitution of the United States by its Founding Fathers in 1776. Oh to the contraire. Wrong Century. Wrong document. Wrong gender.

That distinction belongs to Nina Wilcox Putnam - a writer whose craft ran the gamut from comic books to the silver screen, from romance, musical comedies and westerns to classic of gothic horror.

As a novelist, she penned *In Search of Arcady*, then the screenplay for "Democracy: The Vision Restored, followed

The 1913 Income Tax form designed by Nina Wilcox Putnam

by at least a dozen stories which became motion pictures - among them "Two weeks With Pay", "Graft", "The Fourth Horseman", "Slaves of Beauty" and "Sitting Pretty". With John L Balderston she co-authored the 1927 stage version of "Dracula" and in 1932 co-wrote the story for "The Mummy" Universal's supernatural revenge chiller starring Boris Karloff.

I only learned of Mrs. Putnam's IR$ [sic]connection through a chain of events during production of my feature film, "The Wizard of Speed and Time". My movie's poster was being painted by the legendary Frank Kelly Freas, 10 time Hugo award-winning-science fantasy illustrator and *MAD Magazine* cover artist. With the possibility that this movie venture might produce a tangible income, I asked Kelly's advice on investing. The subject of taxes came up, and Kelly mentioned that he actually knew the person who had created this nations's first tax form.

"She was a heavy woman, about 300 pounds", recalled Kelly, who met Nina Wilcox Putnam through her son John Francis Putnam - a photographer, collector of classical French literature and the first art director at *MAD*. Prior to her book and screen writing career, Nina worked as an accountant. During 1912-1913 she drafted the simple, relatively benign 1040 Tax Form, and set up the whole system. In its first tier was just a 1% tax, and only on those earning over $20,000 per year - a huge sum at a time when a loaf of bread was 5 cents and apartment rent was $12 a month. It's reported that she and/or congressman wanted to fix a ceiling of 10% on taxation, but that the measure was voted down because "if such a high limit were set, it might someday be met".

Kelly's remarkable story was corroborated by two more world-class legends - the super-prolific satirical cartoonist and linguist Sergio Aragones, who also worked at *Mad Magazine* -and author-agent-publisher-historian-mega collector Forrest J Ackerman, creator of *Famous Monsters of Filmland.*"

May 11th 1916 The J.B. Lippincott Company and Mrs. Putnam were each sued in the Supreme Court for $100,000 in damages by actress and dancer Mae Murray and formerly head of the Mae Murray's restaurant. The plaintiff said she had been libeled by Mrs. Putnam in her book "Adam's Garden published by the J. B. Lippincott.

Robert Putnam died in 1918. The next year she married Robert L. Sanderson, a telephone company official. The marriage terminated in a very public divorce.
(From the New York Times January 9, 1924)

Mrs. Nina Wilcox Putnam Sanderson, novelist will fight the complications arising from her Rhode Island divorce suit and the suit for alienation threatened by Mrs. Ellsworth Bassett of Madison Conn., who alleged that Mrs. Sanderson suggested that she give up Bassett, former clamdigger and now the novelist's literary agent.

In a condition bordering on hysteria and unable to rise from her bed in the Hotel Netherlands, Mrs.. Sanderson yesterday made emphatic denial of Mrs. Bassett's statements. The author denied all wrong-doing and said that publication of the charges had "crucified me, without a chance for a comeback; crucified me with my public" Mrs. Bassett's charges were the result of a jealousy complex," said the writer.

At times her voice was almost inaudible as she rocked herself to and fro, sobbing and pleading her innocence. At other times, anger would get the better of her and she spoke passionately against this :absolutely unfounded scandal." As for the charge that her divorce had be obtained illegally because she had not resided the required period of time in Rhode Island, the author said that she had established a residence there three years ago.

"I have every reason to believe that I had no reason to fear trouble about my residence in Providence. I was absolutely astounded that there should have been any trouble about my divorce. So far as the scandal which Mrs. Bassett has given voice to goes, I cannot understand what caused her to make such extraordinary statements.

"I was absolutely overcome by the astounding scandal which has arisen against my name. If I have ever stood for anything in this country it has been for home and marriage. I still believe in it firmly. I am absolutely against divorce and do not believe that it should be reverted to, except in cases of absolute necessity. As far as that matter is concerned I have acted on, the advice of my attorney.

"I hope my public - -" and here Mrs. Sanderson broke into unrestrained sobbing ~ "If I have any, will believe that I have done nothing except what I believed to be right."

She was asked about the midnight interview charged by Mrs. Bassett, at which the novelist and Basset suggested that the young wife enable the erst-while clamdigger win his freedom.

"There never was such a meeting," said the author, "We never discussed it. They called one evening, but it was purely a social call."

Mrs. Sanderson told how Bassett came to enter her employ. After a serious illness, she said, her physician told her that she would have to give up driving her automobile. The doctor suggested Bassett, a neighbor, as competent ti take the job. Bassett, who had turned from clams to house painting, was engaged. Mrs. Bassett continued the writer, participated in the engagement of her husband and appeared to think that the arrangement would be most welcome to the Bassett family chequer. Eventually, on Basset's plea that he be given a chance to get on in the world, Mrs. Sanderson appointed him a sort of literary business agent.

At the height of her career in the Nineteen Twenties Mrs.Putnam was one of the most highly paid woman writers in the United States.In 1925 the New York Times reported that on October 18th while driving to her winter home in West Palm Beach Florida, with a friend, R.W. Gauger, they were involved in a minor car accident and while they were trying to fix the car, Five armed men accosted them and took $6,000 in jewels and cash. The identity of the robbers was never discovered. It wasn't much quieter in her home town New Haven, Conn..When State Senator Arthur Marsden was divorced from his wife it brought Mrs. Putnam back in the by-lines: "When Marsden was attacked by the State Republican organization three years ago, Nina Wilcox Putnam wrote articles in dialect to New Haven newspapers defending his political career. Later he defended Mrs. Putnam's chauffeur, who was accused by his wife of being too attentive to his employer and who separated from him on that account"

Her popularity remained intact, and her humorous stories appeared regularly in such publications as The Saturday Evening Post. She estimated at one time that she had made a good deal more than $1,000,000 out of her writing.

During the 1920s she also wrote a syndicated newspaper column "I and George" which appeared in over 400 papers. Some of her most popular stories were written in an easy slangy manner and bubbled over with her gaiety and laughter. She never took her writing seriously nor did any of the critics. Her other writings where of the more zany aspects of suburban life, of women who struggled to keep their weight down - -a struggle which she shared from time to time - - and of people getting mixed up in funny messes while traveling or while in love.

In 1931 she married Arthur James Ogle, a Florida real estate man but they also divorced a year later.

In 1933 she was married again to an Englishman named Christian Elliot. Mr. Elliot passed away and she outlived him by many years.

On November 14, 1933, Nina Wilcox Putnam, author, Beverly Hills, filed a voluntary petition in bankruptcy court today, scheduling liabilities of $12,136 and assets at $1,977. The only exemption claimed by the writer was $75 worth of wearing apparel and a $72 equity in a bedroom suite. Listed in her assets was her interest in the copyright of three books.

She left the United States and moved to Cueravaca, Mexico where she bought a hotel - originally the Bishop's Palace, built over an Aztec pyramid - and retired in one of its apartments. She died there on March 8,1962 at the age of 77. At the time she was survived by her son and three grandchildren

Among the books by Mrs. Putnam were "In search of Arcady," (1912); "The Impossible Boy" (1913); "Adam's Garden" (1916); "Sunny Bunny," (1918); and "Winkle Twinkle Twinkle and Lollipops (1918); Lynn, Cover Girl, (1950).

Films based on her stories and scripts: *Graft*, (1915); *The Price of Applause* (1918); *It's a Bear* (1919); *In Search of Arcady* (1919); *Democracy, The Vision Restored* (1920); *Two Weeks with Pay* (1921); *A Game Chicken*, (1922); *The Beauty Prize*, (1924); *The Beautiful Cheat*, (1926); *Slaves of Beauty* (1927); *The Fourth Horseman*, (1932), *Cagliostro, King of the Dead* (1932), *The Mummy*, co author, (1932); *A Lady's Profession* (1933); *Golden Harvest*, (1933); *Sitting Pretty*, (1933)

Turgeon. 1942
Nina Wilcox Putnam

Editor's note - Being Historic Film Documents the treatment and script are presented exactly as presented in 1932 including typo's and punctuation. According to Carl Laemmle Jr this film projecd was originally conceived with Bela Lugosi in mind but early-on changed to a Karloff project - PJR

"CAGLIOSTRO"

(Synopsis for a proposed original
script, based on the life of the
famous Italian magician of that
name,)

by

NINA WILCOX PUTNAM

T H E   C A S T

Senor Cagliostro . . . . The Man who lived
                                          three thousand years.

Helen Dorrington . . . . The Girl

Mrs. Dorrington . . . . Her invalid mother.

Dr. Jack Foster . . . . The Boy

Mr. Llewellyn . . . . A Lawyer

The Black Shadow . . . . Cagliostro's servant,
                                         a giant negro.

Mr. H.C.H.Whemple . . . . The murdered
                                         millionaire

Professor Thernley Whemple . . . . Noted Archaeologist,
                                       brother of the
                                       murdered man

Carlton Oews . . . . Head of the Trust
                                       Department at The
                                       Ocean Bank & Trust
                                       Company

Chief of Police . . . .

Ratty Ryan . . . . .The Stool Pigeon

MAIN SITUATION

Through learning the secrets of the ancient Egyptian priests a man has lived for three thousand years, without changing in appear since his thirty-fifth year. In his real youth he was betrayed by the woman he loved and since then, through the centuries, each time he sees a young girl who resembles her, he seeks to posses her and then destroy her out of revenge. His great intelligence has made it possible for him to keep ahead of scientific inventions. He knows all the charlatan tricks better than Houdini or the Indian fakers.

The use of radio and television for purposes of robbery and murder, as indicated in this story, are scientifically possible, and he has improved radio-television to a point where he can project or receive pictures by radio to any desired spot, without a receiving-machine being necessary at this objective. In connection with the radio, he uses a death-ray of his own invention which paralyses the hearts of his victims. His wealth is replenished by apparently supernatural thefts. In his endeavour to trap a modern young girl, he is destroyed through lack of the nitrate injections which keep him alive and he crumbles to a handful of dust, leaving her safe with her young doctor-sweetheart.

SYNOPSIS

San Francisco, winter of 1932. A Japanese Liner from the Orient comes into the harbor during a dense fog, bearing a strange passenger, a blind man and his negro attendant. In their cabin is a curious machine—a super-radio, which greatly occupies them. In the blind

Cagliastro

man's possession is also a curious illuminated portrait of a young woman, an early Egyptian miniature itaglis. This portrait resembles the girl, Helen Dorrington.

A short time before the arrival of the steamer, H.C.H. Whemple, houses on Nob Hill—the largest, finest mansion in the city, and a house which was built by him under sealed orders. The house not only commands an extra-ordinary view of the city from all sides, but it is reputed to be a sort of stronghold, as old Whemples had a fear of burglars which amounted to a complex. Never the less, while in perfect health and only two hours after he had been examined by his physician, young Dr. Jack Foster, and pronounced in fine shape, he had been found dead from a strange form of heart disease, a type so completely unknown that your Dr. Jack insists death was caused by some outside agency. The body was found in a room where doors and windows were both locked from the inside. Search of the panelled walls failed to reveal any secret mode of entrance and in the end the coroner's jury returned a verdict of death from natural causes. Whemple left only one relative, a brother, who was a distinguished archaeologist, head of the local museum, but the will disclosed the brother had been cut off with a dollar, owing to an old quarrel. It seems the millionaire, being very religious in an ignorant way, resented his brother's archaeological researches as sacrilegious. A bitter enmity had thus arisen between them and the brother is rather suspected of causing the death. The property has been left in trust to young Doctor Jack, who cannot touch any of it until he is thirty years of age, in six month's time. A bank sets as executor.

Cagliastro (sic)

Dr. Jack is deeply in love with Helen Dorrington. The Dorringtons were once social leaders in San Francisco, but after the crash her father died, and her mother became an invalid and they are absolutely penniless and very proud. At least the mother is so proud that she makes things very difficult for her daughter, who face once graced all the rotogravures, and was known on her debut as society's favorite. Now the girl is working as ticket-seller at a small movie house on Front Street to support the mother. Helen loves Dr. Jack but will not accept help from him. In fact he can't offer much since Mr. Whemple was his only wealthy patient and Whemple's strange death has hurt him professionally. He now has a hard time supporting himself, pending his inheritance, as no provision was made in the will for any allowance.

Helen and Dr., Jack, however, have a good a time as their limited means will allow—lovers can get a lot out of a cheap Italian restaurant dinner if it is eaten together, and a bench in the park under a full moon has served other lovers before them. Incidently, the radio brings the lovers dance music in her humble flat, and great concert music to which they listen, heads together on the sofa before her fire. D Dr. Jack is a radio fan, and an expert radio-man. It is his hobby. In spite of Jack's free medical attendance, the mother grows worse. It is absolutely necessary for her to have comforts they cannot give her. Helen saves and scrimps and goes without her lunch in order to have extras for her mother, but it is not enough. Both Helen and Jack are in despair about the necessary funds when one day Helen receives a letter from a lawyer, Mr. Llewellyn, asking her to call at his office. She goes to the magnificent office suite and is told her father's younger brother from Australia is looking for her; he is blind, alone

Cagliastro

in the world and enormously rich—will she take pity on him and come to live with him? He has rented the fabulous Whemple mansion and lives there alone with his colored attendant. Excited, she returns to her mother, who confirms the fact that her dead husband did have a younger brother—supposed to be a worthless scoundrel who died years ago. The girl goes to see her uncle and is admitted by a giant negro, who apparently cannot speak. The house is neglected —the great hall and drawing room cob-webby and dusty—but the large library, a circular room in a tower, is warm, lighted and comfortable—and there is the "uncle" helplessly blind, playing with this radio (an uncommonly large and handsome one) as any blind man might. During their interview the uncle makes only one condition—she must not bring her mother to live with them, as he cannot endure sick people in the house. But he will give her unlimited wealth with which to provide for her mother's needs. The girl feels something uncanny about the house, but tries to laugh it off—she is too desperately poor to have any choice in the matter—so she moves in. In waiting on her uncle, which she dislikes doing, she notices that wherever he has been there is dust— an unpleasant dust on the arm of his chair, on the cushion where his head has rested, etc. She has never seen his bedroom—and it slowly dawns on her that she has never seen him eat. As a matter of fact he takes an injection of some kind which he himself prepares. Helen has brought her pet dog to the house with her—a lovely dog. When the dog catches sight of the uncle, his bristles go up and he snarls. The uncle, showing terror of a mentality he cannot control, orders the dog out of the house, but Helen for once standing on her rights, refuses, and next day the dog is dead—of heart disease.

Cagliostro

As us only natural Helen suggests that perhaps Dr. Jack could cure her uncle's blindness. She invites Jack to the house without permission, with the end in view. But the uncle is furious—won't allow Jack anywhere near him as soon as he senses that Helen is interested in Jack, and forbids Jack the house.

Meanwhile an extraordinary series of robberies and deaths have begun to take place. The safety vault of The Ocean Bank is robbed—an unheard of occurrence, since it was considered absolutely invulnerable. The doors have simple been opened without injury and a vast sum in c ash is gone. Both watchmen are dead—of heart disease. As in the case of Mr. Whemple, there is no indication they died of fright, and no organic disease to account for death. The heart has simply congealed— the valves frozen and ceasing to function as though filled with ice. Only one witness was near the scene of the crime and this person claims to have seen the shadow of a giant negro on the blind of the bank. Dr. Jack, called in by Professor Whemple, (who is still somewhat under suspicion in connection with his brother's death) examines both bodies, but cannot solve the mystery. The professor, who is now devoting his life to clearing his own reputation, takes Jack to his house, asks if he has seen Helen's uncle, his tenant? Yes he has. The Professor shows Dr. Jack and 18th century portrait of Cagliostro, the great Italian magician of whose death there is no account. (Note: Cagliastro, the magician, is supposed to have solved the secret of longevity and is an actual historical character. He was much feted at the court of Louis XV) The Professor points out that Helen's uncle bears a startling resemblance to this portrait. He then tells Cagliastro's history—of the beautiful girl who deceived him, and of how Cagliastro went through the centuries, getting his clutches on every girl who

Cagliostro

resembled her, ruining her, and then killing her by slow torture, in
unholy revenge on all womankind. Where does the uncle get his wealth,
the Professor asks? Nobody can find out, but he spends with
extraordinary lavishness. The same was true of Cagliastro. The
Professor then shows Dr. Jack a lot of evidence among his a archaeological
data, to prove that through the centuries people have believed the
secret of eternal youth could be found—there was Merlin, the great
English sorcerer of the 13th century—before that the Priests of
Osiris in Egypt, who knew how to preserve the body indefinitely and
were suspected of supernatural powers. The Professor points to the
legend on the Wandering Jew, and many other instances of characters
who were credited with defying the laws of God and man and living
forever—What a monster such a creature could become! The Professor's
claim is that modern science is the only half-baked and touches only the
obvious, whereas there are all sorts of elements such as "ghosts" and
other "supernatural" things which are really perfectly natural, but
so far unclassified by scientific research and consequently abused by
those who stumble on their potentialities and use them unscrupulously.
He claims the "uncle" is such a character—perhaps worse, a physical
phenomenon. The young doctor is unconvinced, but disturbed by this
thought—and is not reassured when next day Helen tells him that in
the middle of the night she awoke to find her uncle standing at the foot
of her bed, a weird light around him, his eyes blazing at her lustily.
She screamed and he vanished, but when she switched on the light and
sprang from her bed, through the room was empty, on the footboard of
her bed were two dusty hand prints where he had been leaning! When
she came to her senses she realized she'd seised a little crucifix
she always kept by her bedside, and is holding it. Dr. Jack begs

Cagliostro

her to leave the house at once and she promises to do so. He does not believe all of her story but is afraid she's in for a nervous breakdown.

Helen goes to her uncle in the big circular room and tells him she is going. He apparently permits her to go, but the negro, at a signal, shadows her to her room. She sees his shadow and faints. The negro picks her up and carries her to the cellars and locks her in, still unconscious. When she comes to she is a prisoner, she does not know where—the walls are stone and very thick—but she has a horrible feeling that she is being watched. And she is—by Cagliastro through the medium of his television-machine. Mean while the Doctor is waiting for her with his car, out in the shadows of the great house. She does not come and he gets worried. He goes to the door and the negro tells him she left sometime ago. So Dr. Jack goes away, looking for her at her mother's. She is of course not there.

That night Professor Whemple's house is robbed and the portrait of Cagliastro is among the missing articles. Also some valuable data on longevity. Nothing else has been touched, but the Professor has seen the Black Shadow of the giant Nubian on the window—the same shadow which has followed every murder and robbery in the past few months. The police are making a wide search for this negro, and cannot find him or anyone the least bit like him except the Blind-man's attendant. who, it is absolutely proven, has never left the big house since his arrival. His shadow has of course left it, projected by television, in an effort to mislead the police. But the police do unearth the fact that a band of international crooks are in town—a group who have operated successfully in Europe and in Asia at different times. However, nothing can be pinned on them and their leader is, they swear, unknown to them—they have never even seen him, they all declare upon being rounded up and examined.

Cagliostro 8

Then one boy, a weak sister, breaks down under the third degree and lets out that a robbery is planned for the next night—the robbery of a certain vault in a safe deposit, known to the officials to contain nothing but certain precious chemicals. The boy who makes the confession palpably does not know what they are to steal and thinks it is money. But the police, knowing the nature of the contents of the vault, are puzzled. On his promise to act as stool pigeon, the boy member of the gang is released. Then the Chief sends for Professor Whemple, with whom he has been associated over his brother's mysterious death. The Chief asks the Professor what the latter thinks of such a robbery? anyone who had taken the trouble to discover what the vault might contain must want the contents for a peculiar reason. The vault contains nitrates and other life-prolonging chemicals in condensed form. The Professor is intensely interested, but when the Chief invites him to shadow the gang to the scene of the proposed burglary, he refuses.

The next night the Professor, who is familiar with his dead brother's peculiar house, gains access to it by a secret entrance. He creeps in and examines the place. In a hidden cupboard at the head of the carved bed in which the master of the house sleeps, the Professor finds a set of hypodermic syringes and a substance which he recognizes as being part of the formula supposed to have been used by the Priests of Osiris, by Merlin, by Cagliastro, etc., for indefinitely prolonged the preservation of the human body. It is plain that this outfit belongs to Helen's supposed uncle. Trembling with excitement the Professor confiscates the whole layout for future analysis, puts it in his pocket and steals through the ghostly house until he reaches the circular library in the tower room. There he finds the creature, Cagliastro, in the very act of guiding the robbery by means of his radio.

Cagliostro

The "uncle" is so deeply absorbed by what he is doing that the Professor sees the whole operation. The machine is not a harmless ordinary radio, as first appears, but a television-machine as well, by which the operator is enabled to see anything he wishes. At the moment of the vision is centered on the outside door where the robbery is to occur. The watchman comes into sight on the screen: Cagliastro, turns on a death-ray, and the watchman drops dead. Then Cagliastro speaking in an ordinary voice into some sort of microphone, informs the waiting gang-leader that the coast is clear. Plainly his method has been to instruct his gang by radio only, the leader carrying a small receiving set, and getting the message in code, both as to when and how the robbery is to occur, and where the loot is to be placed for collection by the negro. It later comes out that any who failed to obey these orders were destroyed by the death-ray.

Overcome by horror at what he sees, the Professor inadvertently makes a sound. Cagliastro, who is not blind at all, whirls upon him and, with the e aid of the negro, overcomes him., and the Professor is thrown into the cellar adjoining that which Helen is hold a prisoner. The Professor hears her sobbing, and communicates with her, but cannot get to her.

Next morning the town is agog with the new murder which was accomplished under the very eyes of the shadowing police. The robbery was not completed, owing to the interruption of Cagliastro" signals. But the Professor has now disappeared. He was last seen in company of Dr. Jack, so the Chief sends for Jack who tells him about Helen's disappearance. The police, lead by Dr. Jack, storm the house on the hill. Inside it, the giant negro holds the door while his master, wild-eyed and slowly decaying before the Black's very eyes, searches

Cagliostro   10

wildly for the hypodermic, without which he cannot live. Failing to find it in the bedside cupboard, he falls feebly on the bed. The door is broken, in the Black goes raving mad and is overpowered The two in the cellars, Helen and the Professor, are rescued, but Cagliostro has disappeared. On his bed his clothing is discovered, lying as if it had once contained a man, but inside is nothing but a few handfuls of dust—the sort of dust to which Egyptian mummies crumble when exposed to the air.

The Professor demonstrates that his brother was killed by the deathray, operated by Cagliastro from the e incoming ship, because the house suited his purpose and he wanted it to be available. The Professor is cleared and the lovers are united.

                                                                        THE END

This project came not from a published novel or a Broadway play but out of the imagination of Nina Wilcox Putnam. Several projects were planned for Boris Karloff after his success in *Frankenstein* (1931) based on the book my Mary Wollstonecraft Shelley and the play by John L. Balderston.

Carl Laemmle Junior was trying to build Karloff up as a new Lon Chaney (who had died the previous year, leaving a great void in macabre movies). It was announced in the Universal Exhibitor's Book for 1932-1933 that Karloff would portray The Invisible Man and Cagliostro, The King of the Dead. It was rumored that a treatment for *A Trip to Mars* was another project and Robert Florey had written a script for a Karloff entitled The Wolfman 10 years before it was made famous by Lon Chaney Junior.

For once both Carl Laemmle Sr. and Jr. agreed. Neither cared for science fiction films; with the exception of Metropolis and that was only because it was made by Sr.'s friends at UFA Studios in Germany.

The first treatments of Cagliostro where science fiction involving some metaphysical themes, a radio-television death machine and teleportation devises which allowed Cagliostro to project himself to scenes of bank robberies and jewelry heists. Interesting, but no monster. So the project was turned over to John L. Balderston.

In 1925 Balderston, was a distinguished correspondent for the New York World newspaper, and was one of a select few journalist to accompany Howard Carter, the discoverer of the tomb of Tutankhamun (1922). Carter, had been forced by the Egyptian government to wait three years before permission was granted for him to return to the tomb and catalog the contents.

(From Eloise Ross Rubincam's fascinating articlefor FilmFax magazine, Issue 87-88, October of 2002):

"The supreme moment of all archeological research was reached "with" "the merest hint of the unimaginable splendors revealed when the crown jewels of ancient Egypt were brought to light before an awed little group." JLB

"Embalming fluid had so soaked through the bandages that it caused them to adhere to the body" he wrote, "and they have to be cut away in chunks, an operation of supreme delicacy if injury to the flesh is to be avoided." JLB

The script in Balderston's hands was changed to Im-Ho-Tep and all of his first hand knowledge of the contents of Tut's tomb brought an authenticity to the script. He even included scenes where a "Curse" is referenced.

The Laemmle's were pleased with the new script but not the title, still no monster. An inner office memo went out offering $50 to whoever came up with a proper title. The Mummy won and Cagliostro would have been long forgotten had not Carl Laemmle Jr saved Nina Wilcox Putnam's script.

(Above) Boris Karloff, scheduled to star in Cagliostro
(Below) John Lloyd Balderston - screenwriter for Universal Pictures' The Mummy 1932

(From Nina Wilcox Putnam)

"CAGLIOSTRO"

or

(THE KING OF THE DEAD)

Original Screen Story

By

Nina Wilcox Putnam

February 19, 1932

"CAGLIOSTRO"

or

"THE KING OF THE DEAD"

FADE IN

EGYPTIAN SECTION OF THE METROPOLITAN
MUSEUM OF ART, NEW YORK CITY...INT ANGLE

CLOSE SHOT OF A STRANGE EGYPTIAN HEAD. It is the head of a small statuette having the body of a man and the grotesque head of a bird. THE CAMERA MOVES BACK a little to disclose the fact that this figure is one of many in the museum show case. A pair of hands is busy putting those figures in order. cataloging them and pasting little markers on the bottom of them. The first figure is laid in the case, the hands withdraw and then come back to put down a second figure, and then a third. Before the hands lay this third statuette in place they hesitate. CAMERA MOVES BACK to disclose Professor Joseph Whemple, Curator of the Egyptian Department, examining the little figure with interest.

SOUND:
A deep voice which says:
That is not genuine!
Charming but an imitation.

Startled, Joseph Whemple whirls about and faces the intruder. The new comer is s tall, lean man whose cadaverous face is shadowed by a wide brimmed black hat. He wears a long cloak and carries a cane of curious design. This man is Cagliostro, who is known under the name of Dr. Astro

NN

JOSEPH WHEMPLE

>Good God, how you startled me! Where did you come from?

Dr. Astro smiles and indicates entrance with a vague gesture

>Who are you?

DR. ASTRO

>A mere amateur of Egyptology who bows to a great authority like yourself, Signor Whemple.

JOSEPH WHEMPLE

>Yes — I am the curator, but still — I don't understand.

DR. ASTRO
>I have long been wishing to make your acquaintance. But if I may say so without offense, I am surprised that the little imitation Osiris should have crept into your priceless collection.

JOSEPH WHEMPLE

>You make a study of these things, I see

Dr. Astro takes the image from Whemple's hand and points to the back.

DR. ASTRO

>You see this little mark? That identifies it positively as the early part of the reign of Rameses the Third. In the case it is catalogued under Thelmes.

JOSEPH WHEMPLE

>But so are many other objects of Thelmes marked in the same fashion.

DR. ASTRO (SHAKING HIS HEAD AND SMILING)
>I have lived many years in Egypt and I assure you, you are mistaken

JOSEPH WHEMPLE

> May I ask your name?

DR. ASTRO

> Call me Dr. Astro

JOSEPH WHEMPLE

> Ah, so you are the famous mystic! I read in the newspapers about your arrival. You are the chap who can read the future and whom the big Wall Street men are all consulting these days. I'd no idea you dabbled in Egyptology

DR ASTRO

> It's my favorite subject.

JOSEPH WHEMPLE

> It's most interesting. Wait until I get my papers and let us go down to my private office for a chat. It's more comfortable down there. Excuse me just a moment.

Whemple gathers his papers together and busies himself replacing the figure he has taken from the case, etc. CAMERA PANS WITH DR. ASTRO as he approaches the tomb of Iris.

INT. EGYPTIAN ROOM...
CLOSE SHOT OF TOMB OF PRINCESS IRIS:
A FINE   TOMB WHICH HAS BEEN
TRANSPORTED COMPLETE FROM EGYPT

Dr. Astro is standing by the mummy case. It is apparent from his expression that the mummy has some peculiar, tender interest for him. As he stands looking at the mummy —

DISSOLVE SLOWLY INTO:

A SHOT OF DR. ASTRO AND
THE ORIGINAL TOMB OF IRIS

>back to the time when Iris was buried there. We hear the funeral chant of the ancient priests. Dr. Astro in the costume of the period, is chief mourner at the funeral. The funeral services proceed according to the ancient rites of the Osiris including the killing of the princess' slaves who are murdered and thrown into the pit beside her. Their screams partially drowned out by the chant of the priest and the beating of the drums. The funeral party withdraws slowly, leaving Dr. Astro alone with his dead. With a cry of:

>>DR. ASTRO
>>
>>Iris!
>>Iris!

>he throws himself across the sarcophagus weeping, then stands erect with his hand on the carven face on top of the mummy case, the stone covering not yet having been put on the tomb.

EGYPTIAN ROOM IN MUSEUM

>with Dr. Astro's hand still on the face of the mummy case.

CLOSE SHOT OF THE FACE OF THE
MUMMY

>so that it will be easily recognized again.

>Dr. Astro lifts his hand and where it has been there remains a dusty imprint of the palm.

MED SHOT OF WHEMPLE

    approaching Dr. Astro

            JOSEPH WHEMPLE
        Shall we go down now?

Dr. Astro comes to with
a start and joins him.
They exit.

INT...PRIVATE OFFICE ON
THE FLOOR BELOW...MED SHOT

    Dr. Astro and Whemple are
seated at Whemple's desk.
Dr. Astro dim and black
clad with only his dead-
white face distinctly
visible; Mr. Whemple
pink-cheeked, practical,
immaculate and hearty.

           JOHN WHEMPLE
       —so you see, Dr. Astro,
       you really must meet my
       brother. He has been head
       curator of the Museum for
       many years and you will have
       much in common. I know he
       will be astounded by your
       uncommon knowledge and I
       must try to get you together
       soon. Will you dine with me
       tomorrow?

            DR. ASTRO
       I should be delighted!

            JOSEPH WHEMPLE
       Where can I reach you?

            DR. ASTRO
       I'm living at the Waldorf-
       Astoria

            JOSEPH WHEMPLE
       Astrology and mysticism must
       Pay!

            DR. ASTRO
       It does, if you have many
       rich, important American
       clients. It may intrigue you

           CONTINUED

> DR. ASTRO (CONTINUED)
>
> to know that Houdini was
> my pupil, also Thurston,—
> the things I taught them
> were more childish tricks ...
> But it is getting late — I
> must go. Goodnight, sir.

> JOSEPH WHEMPLE
>
> Goodnight, Dr. Astro.

Astro gets up, reaches for his hat and with the other hand leans on a book with a dark binding which is lying on the desk. He then bows himself out. Joseph Whemple glances at the book and sees on it the dusty imprint of Sr. Astro's hand.

We get a CLOSE SHOT of this with Joseph Whemple staring at it incredulously, rubbing the marks with his finger, looking at his hand to show that it is dust that he sees, and then staring incredulously toward the door.

DISSOLVE TO:

MINIATURE LONG SHOT...EXT..PROFESSOR WHEMPLE'S HOUSE ON THE HUDSON PALISADES.

The house is situated on the Jersey shore being on the very edge of the high cliffs overlooking New York. The house has a tower at one end and is built something on the order of a castle on the Rhine with turrets and battlemented top. The garden at the back is surrounded by a high wall, and the house itself is approached by a long flight of steps leading up the cliff from the river.

INT. TOWER ROOM OF THIS HOUSE...NIGHT...FULL SHOT

This is Professor Whemple's combined living room and study. It is a large room with windows on three

NN sides over looking New York City across the river and the country side behind the house. It is richly furnished with antiques, which have been swamped by the Professor's collection of Egyptian treasures which are in evidence everywhere. There is a large work table littered with manuscripts and the room has the air of being much used for study. But tonight the place has a cheerful aspect for the Professor in entertaining. Coffee and liqueurs for five have been set out on a little table near the sofa, and as the scene opens the Professor and his guests are entering the room, coming from dinner.

Dr. Astro, in rather foreign looking evening dress, is the guest of honor. There is also present Dr. Jack Foster, a young physician; Mr. Henry Whemple, Curator of the Metropolitan Museum and brother to the Professor and Miss Helen Barostzi, a young and beautiful girl, who is the Professor's secretary. The group comes down the room, laughing and chatting.

MEDIUM CLOSE SHOT OF THE SAME

> PROFESSOR WHEMPLE (PROTESTINGLY)
>
>> But, Doctor Astro, You've eaten nothing!
>
> DR. ASTRO
>
>> Forgive me but I eat so seldom — and I've had a feast of intelligent conversation.
>
> PROFESSOR WHEMPLE (LAUGHING)
>
>> Indigestion, eh? Well, thank goodness, I have no such troubles.

NN

He turns and slaps Dr. Jack on the shoulder.

        PROFESSOR WHEMPLE (CONTINUED)

    Dr. Foster, here, sees to
    that.

        DR. JACK

    I can back up the Professor's
    statement. He's certainly
    in fine shape.

Astro then notices a fine
fresco on the wall, and
THE CAMERA FOLLOWS HIM as
he goes to examine it
more closely, accompanied by
Mr. Henry Whemple.

Dialogue reveals that Mr.
Whemple is impressed by
Astro's knowledge as they
discuss the period of
the piece.

        HENRY WHEMPLE

    You'd make a fine addition
    to our staff at the museum,
    Dr. Astro. I wish we could
    persuade you to join us.

        DR. ASTRO

    Not just at this time — I'm
    too much occupied with other
    matters. But call upon me
    whenever I can serve you.

Professor Whemple joins them and suggests that Dr. Astro

might like to see the rest of the house. The dialogue

reveals that the Professor has utilized the cellars of

the house to reconstruct the replica of a famous

Egyptian Temple, some portions of the Temple being

the original ones brought from Egypt. Dr. Astro ex-

presses interest and THE CAMERA FOLLOWS the three men

as they move toward the door.

INT. OF THE TEMPLE IN THE CELLARS
OF PROFESSOR WHEMPLE'S HOUSE
(FULL DESCRIPTION OF THIS SET IN
SCENE -5)
FULL SHOT TOWARD ENTRANCE DOOR

> It opens and Astro and the two Whemple brothers come in. CAMERA TRUCKS BACK as they advance, Astro looking about with interest and curiosity as the Professor switches on a light. At this stage, the Temple is empty and undecorated. There are just the columns, the altar and the bare walls. Even the curtains described in Scene M-5 are not yet hung. It is plain that the Temple serves no purpose excepting the preservation of the ancient columns which have been placed there.

MED. SHOT OF THE SAME — ASTRO, THE PROFESSOR
AND HENRY WHEMPLE.

Dialogue shows that Astro is much interested in the room. He then asks Professor Whemple who the girl, Helen Barotzi, is. The Professor explains that he brought her here from Egypt as his secretary. She is the child of an American mother and an Egyptian father who had been left an orphan and penniless in Cairo. Her enthusiastic interest in all things connected with ancient Egypt has been a great asset to Professor Whemple in his research work.

TOWER ROOM — MED. SHOT OF THE SOFA

> on which are seated Helen and Dr. Jack. A short love scene establishes the fact that they are engaged and very much in love. Their love scene is interrupted by the sound of the door opening. They look toward the door

FULL SHOT OF SAME

The three men are returning from their inspection of the house. They come forward and join the lovers. Dr. Astro says that it is getting late and that he must go. They urge him to stay and when he says he cannot, Professor Whemples begs him to return for the week-end. Astro explains that he would greatly like to do so but that it will be impossible for him to see anyone for the next twelve days. He then thanks Professor Whemple for a charming evening and begs him to accept a small souvenir of the occasion. Astro takes out a small charm about the size of a twenty five cent piece, which is attached to a loop of cord. Professor Whemple accepts the gift eagerly.

PROFESSOR WHEMPLE

> Ah, an Osiris, and a genuine one! It is supposed to protect one from all evil is it not?

DR. ASTRO

> I trust it will do so.

Professor Whemple slips the cord about his neck and puts the charm into his vest pocket.

FULL SHOT OF THE ROOM

with Astro saying good-night and Henry Whemple saying; good-night and that he will go with Astro. When the two men are gone, Helen says "good-night" affectionately and goes out, followed by Dr. Jack.

THE TOWER ROOM — CLOSE SHOT OF PROFESSOR
WHEMPLE ALONE

> He is examining the charm under the light of a lamp, the cord still about his neck. He looks at it superstitiously, starts to take it off, then hesitates — his superstition about the good luck omen getting the better of him and he replaces it in his vest pocket and settles down to study under lamp

FADE OUT

FADE IN

INT. OF DR. ASTRO'S LIVING ROOM IN SUITE "A"
AT THE WALDORF-ASTORIA... FULL SHOT...NIGHT

> There is a large and elaborate television-radio machine close to one of the windows. The door from the bedroom opens and a giant Nubian, dressed in Egyptian dragoman costume, enters and crosses the room toward door to outer hall, which he opens as Astro comes in.

CLOSE SHOT OF ASTRO AND NUBIAN

> The nubian bows obsequiously as Astro hands him his hat and cloak. It is evident that he is the magician's slave in spirit if not in fact. Astro instructs the Nubian the he, Astro, is not to be disturbed under any circumstances

FULL SHOT THE SAME

> The Nubian leaves and Astro crosses to where a detailed map of New York is fastened to the wall.

CLOSE SHOT OF ASTRO AT MAP

> locating the house on the Palisades which he has just left. He leaves the map AND CAMERA FOLLOWS him as he crosses to television machine. He seats himself before it and begins to move the dials.

CLOSE SHOT OF THE INSTRUMENT BOARD OF THIS MACHINE

> It is an elaborate affair with intricate dials and illuminated signal bulbs. Astro focuses the machine with care. He shuts off switch marked "television" and turns on switch marked "reverse action". As he turns the switch we hear a curious humming sound and we cut to -

TRICK SHOT OF THE SKY

> showing two zigzag lines of light which converge and form a star which instantly vanishes with a crackling noise.

MED CLOSE SHOT OF ASTRO AT TELEVISION MACHINE

> He adjusts the shutter and we see the screen of the television machine. On this screen appears Professor's house on the Palisades, and then there follows, on the television machine, a series of LAP DISSOLVES as Astro locates what he is searching for with his strange invention. We see the Temple in the cellar of the house, and then the Tower Room with Professor Whemple (where we left him in the CLOSE SHOT on page 11)

NN

MEDIUM SHOT OF ASTRO SEEING THIS ON
SCREEN OF TELEVISION MACHINE

He backs away, rubbing his hands in satisfaction, and CAMERA FOLLOWS him to a nearby cupboard. He unlocks the cupboard door and wheels out a smaller machine. This is a death ray machine which sputters and gives off blue sparks as Astro tests and connects it. He then focuses the death ray machine on the screen of the television.

CLOSE SHOT OF SCREEN OF TELEVISION MACHINE

showing Professor Whemple turning away from the lamp and patting the charm in his vest pocket.

CLOSE SHOT OF DR. ASTRO

with his face close to death ray machine. It is focused to his satisfaction and he pulls a switch on it.

TRICK SHOT OF SKY

with two zigzag of light converging into a star.

INT. OF ASTRO'S ROOMS AT HOTEL
MED SHOT OF ASTRO LOOKING AT TELEVISION MACHINE

CLOSE SHOT OF SCREEN

We see Professor Whemple stagger away from the table clutching at his heart and falling into a heap on the floor.

MED SHOT..THE SAME

> showing Dr. Astro shutting off both machines. He trundles the death ray machine back into the closet, CAMERA FOLLOWING him as he puts it away and locks it up. He turns away from the locked door, puts his keys in his pocket and brushes his hands against each other as though dusting them off. A slight powdering of dust falls from between his palms.

CLOSE SHOT OF DR. ASTRO

> looking at his hands in dismay. We hear the voice of the Nubian:

>> NUBIAN
>> (off scene)
>> The time is short, O Master!

> Astro looks up toward sound of voice.

REVERSE SHOT — THE NUBIAN STANDING IN DOORWAY
BOWING LOW

FULL SHOT OF THE ROOM

> Astro walks the length of the room toward the Nubian, who holds the door to the bedroom open as Astro passes in. the CAMERA FOLLOWING them.

NN
CLOSE SHOT OF NUBIAN AND ASTRO
STANDING BEFORE CLOSED DOOR

    Astro turns to Nubian, makes a gesture with both hands,

    palms upturned — eyes closed.

                  DR. ASTRO

            I am ready. You may begin.

                    FADE OUT

              (PICK UP REVISED SEQUENCE "D")

SEQUENCE "D"

FADE IN:

D-1 PROCESS OR MINIATURE SHOT —
LONG SHOT HUDSON RIVER-TWILIGHT

The shot shows the Palisades on the west bank with Professor Whemple's strange house high on the edge of the cliff overlooking Manhattan. The architecture of the house is ugly and forbidding, being built in fortress style with a stone tower in the manner of a German Medieval castle.

We are approaching it from the water, presumably on the front of a ferry boat, a bit of which is visible in the f.g. immediately in front of the camera. A long flight of stairs leads to the castle, up the face of the cliff from the river.

D-2 MED SHOT OF THE STAIRS
LEADING TO THE HOUSE

Dr. Jack and Police Commissioner Jennings are climbing the stairs laboriously, accompanied by a patrolman and the coroner. CAMERA FOLLOWS them in the ascent. The Coroner, who is fat, is puffing:

> CORONER
> They do pull off these murders in the most inconvenient places. Why couldn't the old boy have got himself bumped off in some place that had an elevator?
>
> JENNINGS
> That is to say, if he was 'bumped off'. The whole business is as queer as this freak house of his.
>
> DR. JACK
> He was in perfect health, I tell you —

They reach the door which is opened by a manservant THE CAMERA FOLLOWS THEM THROUGH

DISSOLVE INTO:

D-3   FULL SHOT OF ROOM WHERE
        MURDERED MAN IS LYING -
        IT IS THE TOWER ROOM

The Professor's body, covered with a sheet, is lying between the radio and one of the big windows, and a cop is sitting not far off smoking a cigar and reading a tabloid newspaper.

CAMERA PANS from the Cop to door which opens to admit Dr. Jack, the Coroner and Commissioner Jennings.

D-4   REVERSE ANGLE

The cop sees them and springs to attention. The men come up to him and the Commissioner nods recognition.

> COMMISSIONER
> Anything new, Casey?

> COP
> His brother is here. He's waiting in the other room.

> COMMISSIONER
> Okay.
> (Pointing to the body)
> Have a look, gentlemen. I'm going in to talk to Mr. Whemple.

The two doctors move over to the body which they conceal as they kneel beside it. The Commissioner crosses to door, opens it and leaves the room.

D-5   REVERSE SIDE OF DOOR

It opens to admit Commissioner who looks across the room and sees Whemple.

> COMMISSIONER
> You are Mr. Henry Whemple?

D-6 REVERSE ANGLE

Mr. Whemple, the curator of the Museum, is sitting by the window, his head buried in his hands. At sound of the voice he rises.

          WHEMPLE
      Oh, the Commissioner, I presume? Yes, I am the brother

The two men shake hands and sit down.

          COMMISSIONER
      Mr. Whemple, we can get the unpleasant matter over if you will answer me frankly and fully. Ahem! Your brother was discovered, I believe, when the maid tried to get in and dust the room and found the door locked. Also, all the windows were closed and fastened on the inside. Is that correct?

          WHEMPLE
      I believe so. Mr. Commissioner, it must have been fright that killed him —a terrible shock of some kind —

          COMMISSIONER
      Ahem — what kind of a shock, Mr. Whemple? What was there in his life that he could have feared?

          WHEMPLE
      I don't know.

          COMMISSIONER
      He must have been afraid of something and been afraid for a long time, or he never would have built such a house as this.

          WHEMPLE
      Er — my brother, Mr. Commissioner, was an odd sort of fellow and resented intrusion here.

(CONTINUED)

D-6 CONTINUED

COMMISSIONER
Did he ever mention any obsession in particular?

WHEMPLE
Well - er - yes, he did have one rather mad notion. It was about the mummies in the collection.

COMMISSIONER
Ummmm —sort of nut, eh? Did you ever think of having an alienist look at him?

WHEMPLE
Yes, at one time we did, but his work in his department was so brilliant that we dismissed the notion.

D-7 DIFFERENT ANGLE

COMMISSIONER
Just exactly what do you mean when you refer to his mad notions?

WHEMPLE
I dislike emphasizing it, Mr. Commissioner, but my brother grew to be afraid of the mummies in his department. Well, it's utter nonsense, of course — but my brother actually believed the things might come to life. Aside from this delusion, he was sane enough, I assure you.

COMMISSIONER
No enemies, eh? How about this young doctor who has been looking after him?

WHEMPLE
Doctor Jack is a friend

(CONTINUED)

D-7 CONTINUED

      COMMISSIONER
   I see.
    (slowly and impressively)
   Did you know, Mr. Whemple
   that your brother recently
   made and filed a will in
   which he left every penny
   of his immense fortune to
   the young doctor?

      WHEMPLE

   Good God, no!

There is the sound of
door opening and both
men look toward it.

D-8 LONG SHOT OF ROOM TOWARD
  DOOR WHICH IS OPENING

The Coroner appears and
beckons.

      COMMISSIONER
    (to Whemple)
   Shall we go?

Commissioner and Whemple
approach the door, the
CAMERA FOLLOWS THEM THROUGH
into the next room. They
join the Coroner. Dr. Jack
is standing near the body
which has now been laid on
a table under the lights.

      CORONER
   It's murder, all right.
   Look at this!

The Coroner leads the way
to the table, followed by
both men. They gather around.

D-9 CRANE SHOT OF A TABLE —
  showing the corpse under a
  strong light, the men's heads
  and hands. The Coroner pushes
  the sheet back from the naked
  chest of the corpse and points

(CONTINUED)

D-9 CONTINUED

    to a small star-like burn directly over the heart. Whemple gasps audibly.

                    CORONER

            A burn — a most curious burn. It doesn't look like anything but a surface injury, yet that's what did it. The muscles of the heart are apparently paralyxed. There's no wound but something —heat apparently —has penetrated clear through. It's the damnest thing I ever saw in my life.

                    DR. JACK

            (picking up small charm with cord attached from table near corpse)

            This was around his neck.

D-10 CLOSE SHOT OF CHARM

    lying in Dr. Jack's hand. Whemple's hand takes it from him.

D-11 MED CLOSE SHOT OF WHEMPLE
     AND OTHERS

                    WHEMPLE

            Why, that was a gift from Dr. Astro! It was supposed to keep the wearer from all harm!

                    <u>FADE OUT</u>

SEQUENCE "E"

FADE IN

E-1 LOBBY OF THE WALDORF ASTORIA
HOTEL   MIDAFTERNOON
MEDIUM SHOT

    showing reception desk with
    smartly dressed clerk behind
    it. Henry Whemple enters
    and approaches the desk.
    Whemple is wearing deep mourn-
    ing and looks care worn.

                  WHEMPLE
              (to clerk)
           Mr. Whemple to see Doctor
           Astro, please.

                    CLERK
           Sorry, sir, but I'm afraid
           Doctor Astro can't be dis-
           turbed. I believe he hasn't
           been very well and he hasn't
           seen anybody for the last few
           days.

                    WHEMPLE
           But I have an appointment —
           made it several days ago.
              (looks at his watch)
           I'm a half hour early. Well,
           call him anyway and let him
           know I'm here.

    Clerk picks up phone

                    CLERK
           Give me Suite A, please .....

DISSOLVE TO:

E-2 BEDROOM OF SUITE A UPSTAIRS
FULL SHOT

    It is a magnificent room
    richly furnished with a
    large, canopied, antique
    bed featured. The room is
    dimly lighted, and on either
    side of the bed are two
    ancient pottery lamps from
    which spring small tongues
    of oil flame wavering in
    the still air. On the bed,
    defined form of a sleeper.
    The coverings reveal nothing

(CONTINUED)

NN

E-2 CONTINUED

except that the form is unusually large and the head is invisible in the deep shadows of the canopy draperies. The decorations of the room are such as to give an impression of mystery and deathly stillness. From the depths of a great arm chair, in which he is at first completely invisible and hidden there arises the form of the giant Nubian. He stands up and is startlingly silhouetted against the lights of the lamps. He is clad only in a loin cloth and turban. He stalks across the room and opens what is apparently an ordinary closet door. The inside of the closet is brilliantly illuminated.

INT OF CLOSET
E-3 CLOSE SHOT

There is a fantastic shrine to the ancient gods of Egypt, Osiris in particular. On the altar, prominently featured, is an hour-glass with the sands in the upper portion running low. The Nubian enters the closet and stands looking intently at the glass for a moment, calculating its speed, and then glances out toward the figure on the bed. He then refixes his attention on the hour-glass. The sound of a telephone bell is heard. The Nubian hears it and leaves the shrine.

E-4 FULL SHOT OF BEDROOM

The Nubian comes in and crosses room to telephone which he answers.

NN

E-5 CLOSE SHOT OF WHEMPLE
SPEAKING ON PHONE AT
DESK DOWNSTAIRS IN LOBBY

> NUBIAN
> No, the master is not yet
> quite ready. It will not be
> until the hour has struck.

E-6 CLOSE SHOT OF WHEMPLE
SPEAKING ON PHONE AT
DESK DOWNSTAIRS IN LOBBY

> WHEMPLE
> But, it's very important that
> I should see him. Don't
> disturb him or hurry him —
> I'll just come upstairs and
> wait.

He hands up the receiver.

E-7 BEDROOM UPSTAIRS
MED SHOT OF THE NUBIAN

putting down phone. He
picks up a burnoose of
heavy silk from a nearby
chair and slips into the
garment.

E-8 UPPER HALLWAY OF THE HOTEL
OPPOSITE ENTRANCE TO SUITE A
SHOWING ELEVATOR   MED SHOT

An elevator comes up, stops,
and Whemple emerges, looks
about him, hesitates a moment
and steps forward seeing the
door he wants.

E-9 REVERSE SHOT   DOOR TO SUITE A

Whemple approaches and rings
a doorbell.

NN
E-10 DRAWING ROOM OF SUITE A
FULL SHOT_____

It is a splendid apartment,
somberly furnished. Featured,
in an unusually fine radio-
television set. Far door
opens and Nubian enters and
crosses room, opens door and
admits Whemple, Nubian bowing
low.

E-11 MEDIUM SHOT
NUBIAN AND WHEMPLE

Whemple looks about him
with an air of curiosity
and interest,-- hands
his hat, stick and gloves
to Nubian.

                WHEMPLE
                (cheerfully)
        Good afternoon. Tell your
        master not to hurry himself.
        I'll just have a look at the
        paper while he's dressing.

He settles himself in a
chair, lights a cigar
picks up a paper and begins
to read. The Nubian bows
and begins to move away.

NOTE: I suggest highly
effective synchronized
music during the follow-
ing scenes.

E-12 BEDROOM MED SHOT

showing the bed and the closet
with its brilliantly lighted
shrine. The Nubian walks into
the picture and enters the
shrine -- stands watching the
hourglass intently. The sands
have all run out.

NN

E-13 CLOSE SHOT OF HOURGLASS

   showing the last grain of
   sand slipping through.

E-14 MED SHOT

   as the last of the sand
   falls, the Nubian springs
   into instant action. He
   leaps into the bedroom
   switching on full lights
   so that the room is brilliant.

E-15 DIFFERENT ANGLE ON ABOVE -
      FEATURING THE BED

   The Nubian approaches the
   bed and with a single gesture
   flings back the coverings
   revealing a mummy case, ancient
   and elaborate. Nubian lifts
   off cover and we see the mummy
   in its stained bindings. It
   looks as if it had not been
   disturbed for a thousand years.

E-16 CLOSE SHOT OF MUMMY

   It writhes slowly. The Nubian,
   who has been bending over it,
   starts back in a horror he has
   never leaned to overcome. He
   then controls himself an,
   slipping one hand under the
   mummy's head starts unwinding
   the wrappings skillfully and
   swiftly.

E-17 DIFFERENT ANGLE ON BED
      MEDIUM CLOSE SHOT OF MUMMY
      CASE

   The Nubian has put the mummy
   back in the case but holds a
   bundle of wrappings in his
   hands. He draws back a trifle
   in awe, gazing steadfastly at
   the mummy case. Then, suddenly,
   the corpse sits bolt upright
   in the mummy case. It is naked
   to the waist, showing a terrible   (CONTINUED)

NN

E-17 CONTINUED
scar where the body was once slit open to remove the intestines. It is a gaunt, thin body, and the flesh is grey-brown and parchment-like, the eyes mere sunken pits of darkness.

DOUBLE EXPOSURE
The erect body slowly taken on human semblance as the air strikes it and the gruesome figure becomes Dr. Astro. Through all this, we hear the subdued whimpering and muttering of the terrified Nubian.
DISSOLVE TO:

E-18 THE BEDROOM
MED SHOT
showing dressing table with Dr. Astro standing in front of it, now his usual self, while the Nubian, better controlled is putting the final touches to his master's toilet. He hands Dr. Astro the cane fashioned like that of Osiris which he always carries, adds the Rosicrucian Cross to his wrist bracelet, dusts off the already immaculate shoes and Dr. Astro, satisfied with his appearance turns from the dressing table. He then gestures to the Nubian to open the door leading to the drawing room and walks toward it.

E-19 DRAWING ROOM
MED SHOT
showing Whemple still reading. He grows tired of the paper, throws it aside, gets up and begins to examine the television machine which is close by. His hand is outstretched to the dials when a voice halts him.

                      VOICE OF DR. ASTRO
                          Don't touch that!
CONTINUED

NN

E-19 CONTINUED
Whemple turns sharply, startled. Then he sees who has spoken and recovers himself

        WHEMPLE
      (heartily)

    Well, well Dr. Astro -
    this is a real pleasure.
    Sorry about the radio --
    marvelous set -- television,
    isn't it? Didn't know it
    was out of order --my
    apologies! Well, sir, I have
    been looking forward to re-
    suming our most interesting
    talk of the other night...

Suddenly his voice trails off into nothing as he senses something uncanny about the man who has just entered.

E-20 REVERSE SHOT SHOWING DR. ASTRO
solemnly regarding his visitor, a menacing figure in his soft black clothing, standing in the entrance door.

        DR. ASTRO
    You have come to speak with me
    about the Egyptian Department
    at the Museum and to ask me
    to take charge of it? Ah,
    that is what I thought. Well,
    my friend, you wish shall be
    granted. In that place I shall
    be at home.

Whemple's expression shows both surprise and relief. He shakes himself out of the horror of a moment before, laughs a little nervously and comes forward.

        WHEMPLE

    You're a mind reader, Dr. Astro.
    Ha! Ha! I'd forgotten for
    the moment that you are a
    noted psychic and you startled
    me. Well, you're right as to
    what I came for.

                CONTINUED

E-20 CONTINUED

                WHEMPLE
                  (continued)
                Then there is the question of
                my brother's house which his
                unfortunate death has left
                vacant. You spoke of wanting
                some place where you could have
                complete privacy. Now, if
                this house would interest you...

They seat themselves an
go on discussing the
proposition as we - -

                            FADE OUT

NN

SEQUENCE "F"

FADE IN:

F-1 THE MUSEUM...INT EGYPTIAN ROOM
NEAR ENTRANCE DOOR. NOON
CLOSE SHOT OF HELEN

in street clothes, renewing
her make-up. She puts away
lipstick and mirror in her
purse, then glances impatiently
at her wrist watch.

F-2 MED SHOT OF SAME

Helen paces back and forth
looking down empty rooms as
though expecting someone.

      HELEN
  Darn Jack! What's delaying
  him?

CUT TO:

F-3 POLICE HEADQUARTERS ..INT
COMMISSIONER'S OFFICE MED SHOT

showing Jennings seated behind
desk. Dr. Jack, wearing his
overcoat and hat in hand, is
seated opposite Jennings. A
couple of detectives are seated
and standing in b.g., being
parties to the examination which
is going forward.

      JENNING
   (continuing)
  --but why should Professor
  Whemple leave you his money?

      DR. JACK

  I tell you, I don't know--
  except he said he was lonely
  and I tried to be good to him.
      JENNINGS

  And you think he found that a
  novelty, eh?

CONTINUED

F-3 CONTINUED

>
> DR. JACK
> Looks that way.
>
> JENNINGS
> Such a novelty that he leaves you, a stranger whom he has only known six months, four million!
>
> DR. JACK
> (indignantly)
> Stop trying to insinuate that I -- I --By God, how could I help his making such a will?
>
> JENNINGS
> Did you know that he quarrelled with his only brother, his only relative, in fact?
>
> DR. JACK
> Yes, his brother tried to prove him insane, I believe.
>
> JENNINGS
> And if it had worked, Henry Whemple would have been appointed guardian of his brother's fortune. Now, in your opinion, Dr. Foster, was the dead man insane?
>
> DR. JACK
> No-o --No, not insane but very high strung and super-sensitive.

F-4 DIFFERENT ANGLE

>
> JENNINGS
> Ummmm -- have your heard that at the time he tried to prove his brother crazy Whemple was badly in need of money?
>
> DR. JACK
> No -- and I don't believe Mr. Henry Whemple capable of such a dirty scheme.
>
> (CONTINUED

F-4 CONTINUED

                JENNINGS
People will do funny things when it comes to money! Well, you understand, Doctor for the present you can't touch a penny of the Whemple fortune. I'll admit we haven't pinned anything on you yet, but you're on probation. You'd better keep where we can get in touch with you at a moment's notice.

CUT TO:

F-5 EGYPTIAN SECTION OF MUSEUM
FULL SHOT

Helen is still alone, waiting for Jack. CAMERA PANS on Helen as she walks down the room examining the exhibit and coming to a standstill in front of an upright case containing the Jewels of Princess Iris.

F-6 MED SHOT OF HELEN

looking into case. A card in the back of the case tells what the jewels are. PAN TO A CLOSE SHOT of the label card and of the jewels which are practical. They consist of necklace, earrings, crown, bracelet and rings. The card reads:

"Jewels found on mummy of Princess Iris Tut-Hekemenn Dynasty of Rameses the Third. H.C. McCary, Upper Nile Expedition, 1932."

PAN BACK TO MEDIUM SHOT OF HELEN fascinated by the jewels.

F-7 FULL SHOT OF EGYPTIAN ROOM

showing door at far end leading into Dr. Astro's private office. The door is closed and Helen's back is toward it. The door is

                CONTINUED

PV

F-7 CONTINUED
flung open violently but
without a sound and Dr. Astro's
sinister figure is sharply
silhouetted against the
light behind him. He sees her
instantly and begins a swift
progress toward her. As he
reaches a midway point, the
CAMERA PICKS him up from a
profile angle.

F-8 MED CLOSE SHOT
showing Dr. Astro in profile
THE CAMERA PANS with him as
he advances rapidly, silently
and eagerly toward Helen, his
face working violently with
emotion. As he comes close
to her we get a MEDIUM CLOSE SHOT
in front of display cabinet
containing the jewels. Dr.
Astro shows recognition -- he
is now absolutely certain of
who she is. CAMERA PANS
to include both Helen and Dr.
Astro, the latter is carried
out of his usual perfect
control.

>	DR. ASTRO
>	Iris! Iris!
>
>	HELEN
>	(turning to him at the
>	sound of his voice
>	startled)
>	Oh! Why, I'm afraid you've
>	made a mistake.
>
>	DR. ASTRO
>	(controlling himself
>	with some difficulty)
>
>	I beg your pardon -- you are
>	very like someone who was
>	once extremely dear to me.
>	I am so sorry -- don't be
>	frightened, please
>
>	HELEN
>	(with a little nervous
>	laugh)
>	Oh, I -- I'm not frightened --
>	not now.
>
>	DR. ASTRO
>	You have seen me before.
>	I am Dr. Astro, the new
>	curator in charge of this
>	department. You met me at
>	Professor Whemple's.

CONTINUED

F-8 CONTINUED

       HELEN
        (doubtfully)

    Of course, That's it --
    here a good deal-- these
    jewels fascinate me. I almost
    feel as if they were mine.

F-9 DIFFERENT ANGLE

       DR. ASTRO
        (lightly)

    Perhaps they were yours in
    some former life. If you are
    interested, won't you let me
    show you my recent gift to
    the collection......

       HELEN
    That would be splendid.

CAMERA FOLLOWS them as they move down the exhibit and pause before a display of some small figures. These objects consist of miniature boats, fully manned, barges with oars, cattle yoked together with their drivers, maid servants, slaves, etc. The figures are about six inches in height, crudely fashioned in clay and brilliantly painted. It is the usual paraphernalia of the Egyptian household. (See designs attached) The objects appear to be crude toys but are really the figures which it was customary to bury with all important personages in ancient Egypt, and represent the personnel which will serve the dead in after life. From this point on through the remainder of the scene, Dr. Astro is using every effort to charm Helen and to gain her confidence

       CONTINUED

PV

F-9 CONTINUED

       DR. ASTRO
      This is the humble contribution
      of which I spoke.

       HELEN
      Aren't they charming! They
      look like toys but I suppose
      they are funeral dolls.

       DR. ASTRO
      Yes, you know they were
      supposed to serve the dead
      in the after life. See this
      little dancing girl?
       (he picks it up)

       HELEN
      How marvelously interesting!

       DR. ASTRO
      I have another figure very
      like her at home. If you
      would care to accept her...
      that is, if it doesn't seem
      to impertinent --my
      offering it on such slight
      acquaintance...

       HELEN
      Oh, I'd love to have it!
      How good of you.

F-10 LONG SHOT OF ROOM
SHOWING ENTRANCE DOOR

 Jack comes in, looks about
 for Helen, sees her and
 advances. His manner is
 troubled and he is rather
 breathless from hurrying.

F-11 MED. SHOT...HELEN AND DR.
 ASTRO.

 still a absorbed in the toys.
 Jack comes into the picture,
 looks searchingly at Dr.
 Astro and Helen
     (CONTINUED)

rh F-11 (CONTINUED)

          DR. JACK

             Helen!

          HELEN
             (startled, as she
             has not noticed his
             approach)

             Why, Jack - -my but you're
             late!. Don't you remember
             Dr. Astro? - - -Just think - -
             he's in charge of the
             department now!

F-12 DIFFERENT ANGLE

Jack, Dr. Astro and Helen.
Jack holds out his hand
as if to shake hands.
Dr. Astro withdraws slightly,
putting his right hand
behind him.

          DR. ASTRO
           (bowing)
           Delighted.

Jack scowls, slightly
puzzled and insulted - -
draws himself up and
puts his arm through
Helen's.

          JACK
           Come , Helen - -Good day,
           Doctor.

          HELEN

           Jack - -don't let's hurry so!
             (as Jacks pulls her
              away - -to Astro:)
           Goodbye!

She waves and smiles
good-bye to Dr. Astro
who stands staring
after her as we - -

FADE OUT

SEQUENCE "G"

FADE IN:

G-1 THE TOWER ROOM OF THE GREAT
    HOUSE ON THE PALISADES
    FULL SHOT... AN HOUR LATER

   It is the same room in which
   Professor Whemple's body was
   found. The room has been re-
   arranged somewhat to accommodate
   the needs of its new tenant,
   Dr. Astro, and his beautiful
   radio-television machine has
   been installed near the large
   windows which overlook the
   city in three directions. On
   the wall opposite the windows
   a detailed map of New York
   City has been hung. Over the
   face of the map a chart has
   been lightly drawn, zoning
   the city into numbered districts.
   Dr. Astro is alone in the room,
   pacing up and down anxiously.
   The door opens and the Nubian
   comes in.

G-2 CLOSE SHOT...DR. ASTRO

                    DR. ASTRO
                    (imperiously)
               Well, have you got it?

G-3 MED SHOT - -

   Dr. Astro standing by table.
   The Nubian comes into the
   picture.

                    NUBIAN
               The master is obeyed.

   From inside his clothing
   he draws out a bit of paper
   and lays it on the table.

NN
G-4 CLOSE SHOT OF PAPER

    on which is written awkwardly,
    as if the writer were un
    accustomed to English letter-
    ing:
        118 E. 22nd Street

G-5 MED CLOSE OF DR. ASTRO
     AND THE NUBIAN

                      DR. ASTRO
                      Good - -you may go now.

    Nubian leaves.
    Dr. Astro picks up paper
    eagerly and CAMERA FOLLOWS
    him over to map on the wall.
    He looks at paper and then
    at map, tracing location
    with one rather dreadful
    hand

G-6 CLOSE SHOT OF ASTRO'S HAND

    showing index finger on the
    location of 118 E. 22nd St.

G-7 CLOSE SHOT OF DR. ASTRO

    marking numerals on a bit
    of paper.

G-8 LONG SHOT OF ROOM

    Astro crosses swiftly to
    television machine

G-9 MED CLOSE SHOT OF ASTRO
     AT THE MACHINE

    It has a very intricate
    instrument board full of
    dials, switches, levers
    and illuminated signal
    bulbs. Astro focuses the
    machine with care. He shuts
    off switch marked "Television"
    and turns on switch marked
    "Reverse Action" as he   CONTINUED

NN G-9 CONTINUED

    turns the switch we hear
    a curious humming sound --

                    CUT TO:

G-10 TRICK SHOT OF THE SKY

    showing two zigzag lines of
    lights which converge and
    form a star which instantly
    vanishes with a crackling
    noise.

G-11 MED SHOT OF ASTRO AT MACHINE

    He adjusts shutter and we see
    the screen of the television
    machine. On this screen appears
    the front of the house
    where Helen lives, then follows
    a series of lap dissolves as
    Astro tries to find a proper
    focus in order to locate the
    exact spot for which his is
    searching.

    LAP DISSOLVE on screen of
    television machine from exterior
    of house to front hall, to
    back room, which is empty, and unfurnished,
    to the room where
    Helen lives. CAMERA MOVES
    up to bed where Helen is lying.

G-12 MED SHOT OF THE TELEVISION
      MACHINE

    with Dr. Astro in the act
    of shutting it off. He has
    now seen all he needs to and
    he is inordinately pleased.
    He folds his hands over
    one another expressing
    satisfaction.

                    DR. ASTRO
                    (muttering to himself)
            At last, Iris, I shall have you,
            and this time you shall not
            die. You will live on forever —
            with me!

NN

G-13 CLOSE SHOT OF DR. ASTRO

    laughing hysterically --
    soft lens -- FULL SCREEN
    CLOSE UP moving right
    into camera.

                          FADE OUT

BG

SEQUENCE "H"

FADE IN:

H-1 CORRIDOR JUST OUTSIDE OF
THE LAW OFFICE OF LEFFINGWELL
AND STRYKER WHO NAMES APPEAR
ON THE GROUND GLASS DOOR
MEDIUM SHOT...EARLY AFTERNOON

Helen and Dr. Jack come
into the picture. They
are wearing street clothes.
Helen carries an open
letter in her hand to
which she refers.

           HELEN
     This must be the place.

They open the door and
CAMERA FOLLOWS THEM into
reception room of the
law offices. A clerk
gets up from the desk
to greet them.

           DR. JACK

     Miss Barotzi has a letter
     from your Mr. Leffingwell..

           CLERK
     He's expecting her. This
     way, please.

H-2 INT. OF LEFFINGWELL'S OFFICE
MED SHOT

The lawyer is a nice con-
fidence-inspiring, respectable
gentleman of middle age. He
is explaining the situation
to Helen and Dr. Jack who are
seated near him.

           DR. JACK
     You say he is a stranger
     in America?

           LAWYER

     Yes, so he thought it would
     be better to have me explain
     his wishes

(CONTINUED)

H-2 CONTINUED

> HELEN
> And you say he is very rich - -
>
> LAWYER
> Most assuredly. He will pay an excellent salary.
>
> DR. JACK
> (to lawyer)
> And just exactly what does this man require Miss Barotzi to do?
>
> LAWYER
> My client asked me to say that besides acting as his secretary, she might undertake to assist him in his research work.
>
> HELEN
> What sort of work?
>
> LAWYER
> Dr. Astro is an Egyptologist.
>
> HELEN
> Dr. Astro! Why, I've met him!
>
> JACK
> Astro! Why, good God, that Charlatan!
>
> HELEN
> How can you call him that? You don't know him.
>
> JACK
> Why everybody has heard of Dr. Astro. I thought his name was familiar. He's just a trick spiritualist or something - - holds seances and does stunts like a regular damned Houdini.
>
> HELEN
> Why I thought he was charming!

(CONTINUED)

BG H-2 CONTINUED - 2

JACK

> (getting to his feet)
> Well, I don't like him at all.
> I don't trust him.

HELEN

> Oh, Jack! I must accept his offer. It's wonderful, his wanting me -- and just now when jobs are so hard to find!
>
> (to lawyer)
>
> Thank him for me, won't you Mr. Leffingwell, and say I'll be glad to come. I'll be there tomorrow

FADE OUT

SEQUENCE "I"

FADE IN:

I-1   PROCESS OR MINIATURE SHOT
      EXT. DR. ASTRO'S HOUSE
      ON THE PALISADES AS SEEN FROM
      THE FERRY BOAT AS IT AP-
      PROACHES THE JERSEY SHORE
      TWILIGHT

      Silhouette of Helen on ferry
      boat immediately in front
      of camera.

I-2   MED SHOT...EXT. FRONT DOOR
      TO THE HOUSE

      Helen comes in and rings the
      bell, and then stands waiting
      to be admitted. She has
      several pieces of luggage which
      she sets down, and she has Max,
      the dog, on a leash. As she
      waits, the glances up at the
      house with interest and
      curiosity. The door is opened
      by the Nubian.

                    HELEN

                         I am Dr. Astro's new
                         secretary.

      The Nubian salaams, gathers
      up her belongings and motions
      her to enter. She does so
      and CAMERA FOLLOWS her into
      a dimly lighted hall where the
      Nubian sets down her bags
      and beckons her to follow
      him. CAMERA FOLLOWS both
      through a dusty and neglected
      reception room and into a
      neglected drawing room where
      cobwebs have fallen on the
      furniture - - on the chandeliers - -
      and the whole room has a chilled
      and forbidding appearance. Helen
      is plainly awed and rather
      frightened, while the dog has
      to be dragged unwillingly on
      his leash. In the far end of
      the room is a curtained door
      leading to a winding staircase.

NN

I-3 CLOSE SHOT OF DOOR
The Nubian pulls back the curtain and motions Helen to mount the stairs. He then tries to take the dog from her but Helen tightens her hold on the leash.

      HELEN
    No, I'll keep him with me.

Helen hesitates slightly and then steps in ahead of the Nubian and goes up the stairs. CAMERA FOLLOWS her to the door at the stairhead, the Nubian remaining below. At the door, Helen hesitates again but finally opens it and goes in.

CUT TO:

I-4 INT TOWER ROOM FULL SHOT
SHOWING ENTRANCE DOOR

Dr. Astro is waiting for Helen. The door opens slowly and Helen enters, looks down the room and sees Dr. Astro.

I-5 REVERSE SHOT

Dr. Astro rises from his chair to greet her, coming forward.

      DR. ASTRO
    Welcome, my dear. It's
    good of you to come to me.
     (Then he suddenly sees
     the dog and draws back
     in terror)
    Take that beast out of here!

I-6 REVERSE SHOT - HELEN AND DOG

      HELEN

    But --but Dr. Astro, Max
    is my best friend.

NN
I-6 CONTINUED

>   DR. ASTRO
>   (deeply agitated)
>
>   Take him out, I say!
>   You can't have a dog.

His eyes are fastened on
the dog with loathing.

I-7 CLOSE SHOT OF MAX

Who has drawn back bristl-
ing and growling

I-8 MED SHOT OF HELEN

soothing her pet,

>   HELEN
>
>   Oh, but please, please
>   don't ask me to give up
>   Max -- I counted on keeping
>   him with me.

Dr. Astro controls him-
self with difficulty

>   DR. ASTRO
>
>   So you like dogs, eh?
>   They are no pets for an
>   Egyptian girl. Besides
>   Rameses would not like it.
>
>   HELEN
>   (bewildered)
>
>   Rameses?
>
>   DR. ASTRO
>
>   The cat. His name is Rameses.
>   He is the sacred cat, mind you --
>   the kind that used to be
>   worshipped.

I-9 CLOSE SHOT OF SLEEK
    BLACK CAT

on a cushion in a sort of
shrine of Egyptian design

NN

I-10 MED SHOT...HELEN AND ASTRO

          HELEN
             I don't like cats very much,
             I'm afraid.

          DR. ASTRO
             Well, we shall not begin our
             new relationship with a
             quarrel. Keep you pet, if you
             wish, my dear, but don't let
             him harm mine.

          HELEN

             That's nice of you.

They smile at each other
and Astro opens a little
casket on a nearby table
and takes out a charm,
exactly like the charm
which was found on Professor
Whemple's body at the
coroner's examination.

I-11 CLOSE SHOT OF CHARM

    in Astro's hand.

I-12 MED SHOT

    Astro gives the charm to
    Helen

          DR. ASTRO

             To cement our good beginning
             I will even present your
             animal with a lucky symbol.
             See - - you put it on his
             collar.

Helen takes charm.

          HELEN

             Thank you. Isn't it pretty?

NN
I-13 CLOSE SHOT OF HELEN

    fastening charm to Max's
    collar. She pats his
    head - - straightens up.

                        DR. ASTRO

              Now, my dear, I want to see
              that you are made quite happy
              and comfortable. You are to
              have everything your heart
              desires.

DISSOLVE TO:

NN

I-14   MED SHOT...TOWER ROOM
       NIGHT

   Dr. Astro is at the television
   machine. He begins to focus
   it.

   DISSOLVE TO:

I-15 HELEN'S BEDROOM IN THE HOUSE
      OF THE PALISADES...FULL SHOT
       NIGHT

   It is a lovely room, gay and
   bright in decoration and has
   a charming painted and canopied
   bed. It is evident that
   Dr. Astro has taken infinite
   pains in preparing Helen's quarters.
   Helen is asleep in the bed and
   only a night light is burning.
   CAMERA PANS from Helen asleep to
   open fireplace before which Max,
   the dog is lying awake and
   watchful.

   DISSOLVE TO:

I-16 TOWER ROOM...MED SHOT

   Dr. Astro is still at the
   machine focusing it. On the
   screen of the machine appears
   the fireplace in Helen's room
   which we have just seen, with
   the dog lying before the fire.
   Dr. Astro gives a smothered
   exclamation of satisfaction.
   He then gets up and going to
   a cabinet trundles out a
   second machine. This is a death-
   ray contraption which sputters
   and gives off blue sparks and
   flashes in the darkened room as
   he connects and tests it. CAMERA
   PANS with Dr. Astro as he moves
   from one machine to the other,
   adjusting the death-ray machine
   so that it points to the dog
   on the screen. On the television
   machine we see the dog turn his
   head and look appealingly right
   at the camera, the charm dangling
   from his collar just below his
   chin, plainly visible. Dr. Astro
   steps back and pulls a switch on
   the death-ray machine.

                                              DISSOLVE TO:

NN

I-17 TRICK SHOT OF SKY

    with two zigzags of
    light converging into a
    star which vanishes   SOUND: dog yelping

I-18 HELEN'S ROOM...FULL SHOT

    showing helen leaping out
    of bed in her night clothes
    and running forward.   SOUND: Dog Yelping
    The sound stops abruptly
    as Helen runs down the room
    into camera.

I-19 CLOSE SHOT OF DOG

    lying before the fire, his
    back to camera. Helen comes
    into picture, kneels by the
    dog and turns him over. He
    is dead and there is a star-
    like burn on his chest.

                        HELEN
                      (weeping bitterly and
                      throwing her arms about
                      the dog's body)

                Max! Oh Max, darling —
                What happened - - what happened?

I-20 TOWER ROOM...MED SHOT

    Dr. Astro is prosaically
    turning off the television
    machine. He then trundles
    death-ray machine back to
    its hiding place.

NN 1-21 BALCONY OUTSIDE HELEN'S BEDROOM
MED SHOT...EARLY MORNING

Full sunlight falls down on a dainty breakfast table set with delicate service for one. There are fresh flowers on the table and a flowering vine is blooming on the balcony rail. In the background is the garden with a mass of apple blossoms against the sunny, cloudless sky. The whole picture breathes freshness, youth and spring. Helen is seated at breakfast in negligee, her hair wind-blown. The dog's collar with the charm still attached are on the breakfast table, as is also a framed photograph of the dog, at which she is gazing as she eats. The Nubian comes into the picture carrying a glittering Egyptian costume and headdress. He bows.

          HELEN
            (a trifle timorously)
          Good Morning.

          NUBIAN
            (indicating costume)

          The master sends these.

          HELEN
          Am I to put them on?

The Nubian nods assent.

          HELEN
          Very well then.

The Nubian starts to leave.

          HELEN
          Wait!

She picks up the dog's collar and framed photograph and gives them to the Nubian.

          Put them on the desk in the
          front which is to be my office.
          Do you understand?

The Nubian bows, takes the collar and picture and goes out.

NN

I-22 DIFFERENT ANGLE

Helen gets to her feet, pushing back the table, takes up the costume which the Nubian has left and throws it over her arm - - then she walks towards the French window leading into her room. At the window she turns back and looks wistfully at the sunlit day before entering the room

CUT TO:

I-23 TOWER ROOM...MEDIUM SHOT DR. ASTRO READING MORNING PAPER

Headlines in paper:
"PROFESSOR WHEMPLE CASE STILL MYSTERY."

He puts down paper and looks up to see:

I-24 REVERSE SHOT

Helen standing before him in her Egyptian costume with the elaborate headdress. She is smiling and very pleased with herself - - like a child with a new toy.

     HELEN
   Well?

I-25 REVERSE SHOT...DR. ASTRO

He gets slowly to his feet and comes toward her with outstretched hands.

     DR. ASTRO

   It is wonderful! Now, you are
   yourself - - your real self!

NN   I-26 MED SHOT...HELEN AND DR.
             ASTRO

             He comes closer to her,
             smiling. He can hardly keep
             his hands off of her. He
             brings his face close to
             hers and looks straight into
             her eyes.

                                            HELEN

                                                 How strange you look!

                                            DR. ASTRO
                                                 I am no stranger to you, child.
                                                 Look! Look well - - don't you
                                                 remember?

                                            HELEN
                                                 (struggling against his
                                                  hypnotic gaze.

                                                 I don't - - I can't - -Oh,
                                                 stop it, please
                                            DR. ASTRO
                                                 (softly)
                                                 Don't you remember, Iris - -
                                                 remember our days together?
                                                 Try Iris! - - those beautiful
                                                 days - - and those soft nights!
                                            HELEN
                                                 (resisting the spell)
                                                 Don't! Oh, I won't remember!
                                                 What are you doing to me?

             Dr. Astro sees that she is
             really frightened and desists.
             He passes his hands lightly
             before her eyes, breaking
             the spell.

        I-27 A DIFFERENT ANGLE
             Helen comes to, still dazed.

                                            HELEN (HALF LAUGHING)
                                                 Why, I had the strangest feel-
                                                 ing. For the moment I thought
                                                 that you - -that I - -
                                            DR. ASTRO
                                                 Forget about that dream. No
                                                 you were not to remember. See,
                                                 you are all right now.
                                                      (his voice changes to
                                                       normal)
                                                 You look charming, my dear. A
                                                 novel business costume, is it not?

NN

I-27 CONTINUED

        HELEN
         (looking at her dress)
         Is this my working dress?
         Why, that seems absurd.

        DR. ASTRO
         But it is not absurd. I
         assure you that the silly clients
         who pay me so well for reading
         their fortune will be greatly
         impressed. Come - - I'll show
         you your new office.

I-28 LONG SHOT OF ROOM

 CAMERA MOVES with them as he leads her away towards the door.

 CUT TO:

I-29 FULL SHOT OF THE RECEPTION ROOM - - LATE AFTERNOON - -

 where Helen has been installed to receive Dr. Astro's clients, to make his appointments and to act as general amanuensis. It is a small room ornately furnished in pure Egyptian style. The walls are covered with dark hangings. Every detail has been carefully carried out to give an impression of antiquity, even the French telephone on the desk being disguised with a carved figure. The only modern note is struck by the collar of the dead dog, Max, which lies on the desk, together with his photograph. Helen, wearing her fanciful costume, is seated at this desk. Altogether the scene is a deliberate piece of good hokum frankly designed to impress the public and it is, in many ways, typical of the reception rooms of charlatans since time immemorial. CAMERA TRUCKS UP TO MEDIUM CLOSE SHOT OF HELEN at the desk. The telephone rings and she picks it up

        CONTINUED

NN   I-29 CONTINUED

>   HELEN
>   Hello...Yes...Who? Oh,
>   Mr. Kingsley of the Banker's
>   Trust Company...Yes...Dr. Astro
>   will see you at ten o'clock
>   tonight...Of course...cer-
>   tainly, your coming will be
>   kept strictly confidential.

Helen puts down the receiver and makes note of the appointment. She hears the door open and looks up.

I-30 REVERSE SHOT...ENTRANCE DOOR

It opens and Dr. Jack comes in. At the sight of Helen's costume he is both startled and amused. He comes forward with outstretched hands.

I-31 MED SHOT...HELEN AND JACK

>   DR. JACK
>   Helen, sweet! Whew, but I
>   had a time getting past the
>   body guard!
>
>   HELEN
>   Jack! Why didn't you phone
>   you were coming?
>
>   DR. JACK
>   I was afraid you wouldn't let
>   me in - -after the way we
>   parted last time.
>
>   HELEN
>   Don't be silly. Of course, I'm
>   glad to see you. Why, it's
>   been almost two weeks.
>
>   DR. JACK
>   Yes - -and without a word from
>   you. I couldn't stand it
>   another minute, sweet - - I had
>   to see you.

CONTINUED

I-31 CONTINUED

     HELEN
      From the tow you made over
      my coming here, I supposed
      you never wanted to see me
      again.

     JACK
      Well, you win. Here I am,
      and please forgive me, dear.
      I didn't mean to fight --
      I was just upset about you
      being in the house.
        (He looks about the room
        curiously)
      You must admit it's kind of
      spooky.

He tries to take her in
his arms but she eludes
him, not unkindly but coolly
rather than coyly. It is
plain throughout the scene
which follows that she is
under Astro's influence and
that she is growing cold toward Jack.

     JACK
      What's the matter, sweet?
      Don't you love me any more?

     HELEN
      Of course, I do, hun -- but
      somehow I don't feel like
      love-making tonight.

Jack drops his hands from
her shoulders, down her
arms and takes her hands,
looking her over.

     JACK
      Gee, that's a pretty costume
      but it makes you terribly
      different, somehow. What's
      the idea?

     HELEN
      It's for the benefit of our
      public. Oh, Jack, you can't
      imagine how many really important people consult dr.
      Astro. I mean really big men.
     JACK - (INDICATING COSTUME
      And do they have to be suplied with this hokum?

             CONTINUED

I-31 CONTINUED 2

          HELEN
          (nodding)
      They are awful children even the big politicians but there's no hokum about Dr. Astro.

I-32 DIFFERENT ANGLE

          JACK
          (shortly)

      Oh! He's wonderful, I suppose.

          HELEN
      He's certainly is. He's the wisest man I ever met. Why, Jack, it's incredible about what that man knows! Not only about ancient things but about modern science, too.

          JACK
      Science, my foot!

          HELEN
      Oh, but he does. He's three jumps ahead of Edison. Look in here a moment.

I-33 MED SHOT AT FAR SIDE OF ROOM

behind Helen's desk, showing an inner door. CAMERA PANS on Helen and Jack as she leads him to the door, opens it part way and beckons him to look through. Inside, beyond the door, is glimpsed a very modern laboratory with the latest equipment, both surgical and electrical. Dr. Jack gives a long, low whistle of astonishment.

          HELEN
          (CLOSING THE DOOR)

      I'm not supposed to let anyone see that but I just wanted to prove to you that he isn't a joke.

      CONTINUED

NN I-33 CONTINUED

>   They move over to desk,
>   CAMERA FOLLOWS them

JACK
> Helen, what's come over you?
> You've changed completely.
> This man has a queer sort of
> influence on you and I don't
> like it.

HELEN
> I admire him, of course.

JACK
> (growing more suspicious)
> Why is he so interested in you?
> Tell me the truth, Helen - -
> has me made love to you?

HELEN
> (shocked)
> Why Jack! He's more like - -
> say an uncle!

JACK
> I don't care. These damned
> Egyptians used to marry their
> sisters - -being you uncle
> wouldn't stop him.

HELEN
> (furious)
> Jack Foster, my father was an
> Egyptian and I won't stand
> here and be insulted!

JACK
> Well, I don't like your being
> here alone with only Max to
> look after you.

> Helen remembers. She picks
> up Max's collar with the
> charm on it from her desk.

HELEN
> Oh, Jack - - Max is dead.

> She shows him the collar
> Jack looks at it and touches
> the charm, frowning.

JACK
> Max dead? What killed him?

HELEN
> I don't know.

CONTINUED

I-33 CONTINUED 2

    JACK

      Damn it all! I don't like
      that either - -this whole
      outfit is wrong somehow.

    HELEN

      Don't be absurd, dear.

    JACK

      Listen, sweet, I'm no such
      thing! And I'll prove to you
      that this man is a faker.
      Good-night!

I-34 LONG SHOT OF ROOM TOWARD
   EXIT

Jack grabs his hat and
stalks out, slamming
the door and leaving Helen
to slowly sink into her
chair dazed by his violence.

        FADE OUT

NN   SEQUENCE "J"

FADE IN:

J-1 TOWER ROOM...NIGHT...MEDIUM CLOSE SHOT OF HELEN reading a large book under a shaded light. She has on an ordinary day dress. Her chair has a low back and the CAMERA ANGLE is from behind showing Astro's arm on the back of her chair and his hand in the foreground. From his wrist dangles the Rosicrucian Cross which he wears on the bangle. Helen's head is bent over the book, her face serious and absorbed in study.

CAMERA PANS TO CLOSE SHOT of book showing open pages with title: "The book of the dead" at the top of the page. There are Egyptian characters and drawings interspersed in the text and in English we read:

"To go in and out of my grave -- to cool myself in its shadow. Even as Osiris is not destroyed, so shall I not be destroyed."

BACK TO MED CLOSE SHOT OF HELEN reading. CAMERA TRUCKS BACK to include Doctor Astro, seated beside Helen, explaining the nature of the book. He bends over her hoveringly and is deeply solicitous that she understand.

On a table before them are some big volumes with ancient bindings, some rolls of papyrus manuscript of the Middle Ages, Also a modern edition of Plutarch's account of Osiris and Isis; also some modern scientific books

                     DR. ASTRO
              No death --you understand
              the first principle of life is,
              that there is no death!
                     HELEN
              Even back in the time of Osiris
              they believed the body could
              go on indefinitely, didn't they?   CONTINUED

NN   J-1 CONTINUED

> DR. ASTRO
> My child, you must first clear your mind of the thought of mummifying as an end in itself. What I am trying to explain to you is that suspended animation was practiced by the Rosicrucians as early as the building of the Temple of the Twelve Cells
>
> HELEN
> (protesting)
> But - - but - -
>
> DR. ASTRO
> (interrupting)
>
> Suspended animation is not a phenomenon. It is the most natural thing in the world. A simple scientific fact.
>
> HELEN
> (reaching out and taking up the volumn of Plutarch)
> And here Plutarch says the Ka, or animation, shall re-enter the body at intervals - - Do you really believe that?
>
> DR. ASTRO
> Yes, and furthermore the soul can be transferred from one body to another. But first the mind of the subject must be prepared - - carefully - - slowly - - through conviction . . . .

Helen's eyes are fastened on his face in rapt attention. It is evident she is a willing pupil, eager to learn - - willing to submit to his superior knowledge

DISSOLVE TO:

J-2   EXT. OF A FINE PRIVATE MANSION...AFTERNOON... MEDIUM SHOT . . . . .

This is Henry Whemple's home. Dr. Jack comes up the steps and rings the door bell

DISSOLVE TO:

-90-

J-3 LIVING ROOM OF THE HOUSE MED SHOT

showing door from hall. Henry Whemple is seated in a large easy chair. He wears a smoking jacket and is reading a learned looking book. Other volumes suggestive of research are piled beside him on the floor, and on a smoking stand by the chair is a heap of manuscript, old and much handled. Mr. Whemple is seated in front of a cheerfull open fire and above the mantel piece is a fine Eighteenth Century life sized portrait of a man. This portrait is only dimly discernible at present. The room is furnished with antiques in a well chosen conglomeration such as a distinguished and wealthy collector might possess. Mr. Whemple's taste evidently runs to Eighteenth Century French and Italian pieces.

The door is opened by a butler, who announces

          BUTLER
     Mr. Foster is here, Mr. Whemple.

Whemple, startled from his reading, looks up.

          WHEMPLE
     Eh? Foster? Show him in.

The butler stands aside and Jack enters. He has left his hat and gloves in the hall and was evidently expected.

          JACK
     Good afternoon, Mr. Whemple.
     I hope you won't mind my
     calling up for this appointment.

          WHEMPLE
     Not at all, young man, not at
     all. Sit down

NN

J-4 CLOSE SHOT OF WHEMPLE AND JACK

> They seat themselves before
> the fire.

JACK
   I was a trifle afraid that
   because of your brother's
   will you might.....

WHEMPLE
   No, Dr. Foster -- on the
   contrary I appreciate that
   the will in your favor has
   done me more good than harm.

JACK
   How's that?

WHEMPLE
   The damn police are still
   watching me with suspicion --
   and if I had inherited
   matters would be worse.

JACK
   Ah, I see. I suppose no new
   clue to the professor's
   mysterious death has been discovered?

WHEMPLE
   None, I regret to say. But
   let's not talk of that, please
   What was it you wanted to see
   me about?

JACK
   About the tenant in your late
   brother's house.

WHEMPLE
   Dr. Astro? The other
   executors wanted to rent the
   place and as I know Dr. Astro
   wished for privacy --

JACK
   (interrupting)
   That's just it. There's too
   much privacy over there. Helen
   is living with him, you know,
   and something is wrong.

WHEMPLE
   Wrong? What's wrong?   (CONTINUED)

J-4 CONTINUED

>JACK
>Well, you see, sir, Helen has changed -- it's not a normal change either. I believe the man is trying some of his damned tricks on her.

>WHEMPLE
>You mean hypnotism?

>JACK
>I don't know exactly what I mean but know things aren't right. Mr. Whemple, you are an influential man. Couldn't you get some important scientist to challenge this Dr. Astro -- to make a scientific test of his powers?

>WHEMPLE
>You want to show him up, eh?

>JACK
>That's about it. Of course I'll admit it's Helen's position that interests me, but just the same the man is a notorious faker.

J-5 MED SHOT

Jack gets up and begins pacing the room as he talks. Whemple gets up and stands with his back to the fire.

>WHEMPLE
>Why, my dear chap -- what do you really know about Astro? Nothing -- except that some of the biggest men in the country think he can read the future. How do you know you can show him up?

>JACK
>(stopping short)
>
>Exactly what do you mean?

>WHEMPLE
>(pointing at the portrait over his head.
>Have a good look at this.

Jack comes closer and stares up at portrait.

-93-

NN

J-6 CLOSE SHOT OF PORTRAIT

It is a three-quarter length painting of a man in knickerbockers, white wig and ruffles. and the face is unmistakably the face of Dr. Astro's.

J-7 CLOSE SHOT OF JACK AND WHEMPLE LOOKING AT PORTRAIT

       JACK
      But it's Dr. Astro!

       WHEMPLE
      No - - it's Cagliostro, the
      great Italian magician - -the
      one Louis XV called to court
      in order to have him transmute
      base metals into gold.

       JACK
      It's the darndest resemblance.

       WHEMPLE
      (quietly)
      Suppose, by chance, it is more
      than a resemblance - - how
      about it being the same man?

       JACK
      Bosh!

       WHEMPLE
      Look here, Foster, until I
      started going over my dead
      brother's notes, I'd have said
      the same thing. Now, I'm not
      so sure

       JACK
      For the love of Heaven, Mr.
      Whemple, why do you say that?

THE CAMERA FOLLOWS them from the fireplace as Whemple leads the way to the books and manuscripts he has been reading when Jack arrived. Whemple picks up a manuscript and turns the leaves as he talks.

       CONTINUED

J-7 CONTINUED

> WHEMPLE
> Where to all these stories of men who have lived hundreds of years--thousands of years, in some cases--come from unless there is an element of truth behind them somewhere?
>
> JACK
> For instance?
>
> WHEMPLE
> I mean the story of the Wandering Jew who is supposed to be still alive, or of Cagliostro, who is supposed to be no less a person than Osiris himself. And how about the Count St. Germain, who is recorded pretty authentically to have lived for seven hundred years?
>
> JACK
> Well, speaking as a physician I'd say that was all absolutely rotten nonsense.
>
> WHEMPLE
> Possibly--but suppose that by chance Cagliostro and this chap, Helen's so-called uncle were really the same? Damned interesting thought eh?
>
> JACK
> (eagerly)
> Then you'll call a conference put him to the test? Will You?
>
> WHEMPLE
> By Jove, I will. I'll have the finest minds in the country to test him and pay him what he likes for the job.
>
> JACK
> (grimly)
> And hold your seance here-- in your own house. That will put him at a disadvantage.

FADE OUT

NN

SEQUENCE "K"

FADE IN:

K-1 EXT. WHEMPLE'S HOUSE
     LONG SHOT.   NIGHT

The house is brilliantly
lighted and a line of cars
and taxis are discharging
guest who have come to
attend Dr. Astro's seance.
Cars move on - -guests
go up the steps and into
front door.

DISSOLVE TO:

K-2 INT OF HOUSE...LIVING ROOM
     FULL SHOT.....EVENING

The room has been re-arranged
to accommodate the gathering
of the wise men. The main
portion of the floor is filled
with camp chairs, most of which
are already occupied by savants
from all over the country. They
are chatting together in groups.
Some have brought their frumpy
wives or sisters with them,
but it is predominately a gathering of men. There are members
of the Society of Phychic Research,
noted doctors, a few statesmen,
a famous preacher or two, a
Catholic priest and a Rabbi.
In shot, an audience well
calculated to strike terror to
the heart of any faker.

As the scene opens the audience
is still arriving, finding seats
greeting acquaintances, etc.
The portrait of Cagliostro has
been removed from its place over
the mantel piece and in its
stead stands a large crystal
sphere. Below the fireplace a
platform has been constructed
and on it stands some of Dr.
Astro's paraphernalia

NN

K-3 MED CLOSE SHOT OF
     THE SAME . . . .

We see a group an animated
spectators near the aisle,
three rows from the front.
The aisle seat is vacant
as is the one immediately
behind it. Dr. Jack comes
into picture and takes this
vacant seat.

K-4 REVERSE SHOT ... THE PLATFORM

This platform is not very
high; just sufficiently so
to enable the spectators
to see clearly. On the platform stand two formal, straight
backed chairs of even height,
a table on which is a large
common earthen flower pot,
a box containing sufficient
earth to fill the flower pot,
a trowel and an ordinary
garden water can filled with
water. On the table there is
also a magician's wand, a short
black baton such as an orchestra
leader uses only shorter. Just
behind the platform to the right
is a door leading from the next
room - -the same door though which
Jack came on the occasion
of his visit to Whemple. This
door opens and Whemple comes in.
He mounts the platform
and holds up his hand for attention.

    SOUND: Applause and voices which
       die down to a murmur
       and then silence.

    WHEMPLE
     Ladies and gentlemen!
     We are here tonight to test
     the powers of the most
     famous psychic of our time.
     It is a serious occasion
     which should prove of great
     interest to all of us.

NN

K-5 CLOSE SHOT OF WHEMPLE
    ADDRESSING AUDIENCE

                WHEMPLE
        Dr. Astro claims not only
        to be familiar with the methods
        of Messer, Gassner and Casanova
        but with those employed also
        by Madame Blavatsky and other
        leading spiritualists. He is
        also going to show us some of the
        magic of the orient. These
        'tricks', he asserts, have
        actually a supernatural element
        in them. It is Doctor Astro's
        assertion that science, as
        most of us here understand it,
        discounts these phenomena through
        ignorance of their real nature.
        It remains for Doctor Astro to
        convince us. It also remains
        for us to prove him wrong. We
        invite your closest attention to
        his demonstration.

Whemple turns toward the
door though which he
entered, and which is
still slightly ajar, and
raising his voice slightly
calls: Doctor Astro!

Whemple steps down from
the platform and out of
picture.

DISSOLVE TO:

K-6 LONG SHOT OF ROOM

towards door behind plat-
form, heads of audience
in f.g. as they crane
their necks to see Astro's
entrance.

The door opens and Dr. Astro
comes in wearing beautiful
evening clothes and a long
full cloak. He carries his
curious cane and advances
slowly into the room, followed
by the Nubian. The Nubian
wears a turban and a long
close-fitting Egyptian coat,
belted with a sash, the typical
dress costume of a Dragoman

                                                  (CONTINUED)

K-6 CONTINUED

As they approach the
platform, the CAMERA
TRUCKS up to MEDIUM SHOT.
Dr. Astro slips his cloak
from his shoulders and
the Nubian takes it. TRUCK
UP to FULL CLOSE UP of
Dr. Astro looking at his
critical, hostile audience.
His eyes glitter and he
smiles slowly, superciliously,
as if his ancient, superior
wisdom held these critics
in contempt. Then the smile
changes to a polite, con-
ventional smile. CAMERA
TRUCKS BACK TO MEDIUM CLOSE
SHOT of Astro on the platform.
He is bowing politely to the
audience.

> DR. ASTRO
> Ladies and gentlemen!
> Perhaps the simplest and
> most familiar form of
> magic is mind reading.
> So, even as a child learns
> first its ABCs, we will begin
> with a little demonstration ...

DISSOLVE TO:

K-7 FULL SHOT OF THE ROOM
SHOWING ASTRO ON PLATFORM
He is in full action and
his audience is buzzing with
excitement. At start of
shot a wise-looking, white-
headed professor is getting
to his feet in the midst
of the crowd. As Astro's
voice is saying

> ASTRO'S VOICE
> Next! Next! Who has another
> question?

K-8   MEDIUM CLOSE SHOT
of the gentleman who has
stood up. He raises his
hand.

> THE GENTLEMAN
> I'm thinking of a mathematical
> problem - -can you tell me
> the number of the answer?

K-9   REVERSE SHOT ...DR. ASTRO
ON PLATFORM . . . . .

His hand goes to his fore-head
and he half closes
his eyes.

> DR. ASTRO
>
> your number...Don't bother
> to write it down! The answer
> is 1-4-7-6-0-3, and the problem
> is an astronomical calculation
> concerning the planet Mars.

K-10   REVERSE SHOT OF THE QUESTIONER

who resumes his seat, astonished - -
smiling and speaking to his
neighbor on either hand.

> GENTLEMAN
> That's right. By Jove!
> Got it right.

We hear audible murmur
and exclamations of

> AD LIB
> Remarkable!
>
> Interesting!
>
> A good guess!

from the audience
during the above, but the
audience is still highly
skeptical and taking the
scene rather lightly
according to the sound
effects.

-100-

K-11 MED SHOT TOWARD
     PLATFORM . . . .

and including that
portion of the audience
seated in the first four
rows, also a clear bit of
the aisle. Whemple has
taken seat just back of
Dr. Jack. Dr. Jack leans
back to Whemple and speaks
to him in a low tone.

                        JACK
                    That must have been pre-
                    arranged.--a set of
                    signals.

                        WHEMPLE
                        (bending closer)
                    Get up and ask him something
                    yourself.

He pushes the protecting
Jack to his feet.

K-12 MED SHOT TOWARD PLATFORM

of Jack standing in aisle,
Whemple seated behind him,
neighboring members of the
audience looking at Jack and
Jack looking at Astro.
Astro is facing Jack from
front edge of platform.

                        JACK
                    I have a thought concerning
                    a person in this room--
                    Can you tell me who it is?

Jack steps forward in the
aisle as he speaks and the
CAMERA FOLLOWS him until
he and Astro are both in-
cluded in MEDIUM CLOSE SHOT

                        DR. ASTRO
                    Yes -- you are thinking of me.

                        JACK
                    And in what connection?
                        DR. ASTRO
                        (slowly but not too seriously)
                    You think I am dangerous. You
                    believe I am a criminal, not
                    a scientist, and that I intend
                    harm to someone dear to you.   (CONTINUED)

K-12 CONTINUED

          JACK
            (blurting it out)
          And do you?

          DR. ASTRO
            (suavely)
          Ah, but no! You may not believe it, but any harm to this person is the furthest thing from my mind. Ha - - you are thinking now that you would like to hurt me!

          JACK
          Stop!

          DR. ASTRO
            (smooth and smiling)
          Perhaps, sir, it would be well if you were to stop thinking.

          JACK
            (angry)
          Nobody can help their thoughts, Doctor Astro - - especially when another person's actions make one suspicious.

          DR. ASTRO
          Still, it is unwise to make enemies of those the gods love, because the gods can also destroy.

Jack is angry and his impatience nearly getting the better of him.

          JACK
          That gibberish doesn't fool me, Doctor, or intimidate me, either!

He makes as if to move up on Astro when Whemple comes into the picture and pulls Jack back to his seat, reasoning with and smoothing him in an undertone as we - -

DISSOLVE TO:

K-13 MEDIUM CLOSE SHOT
OF ASTRO ON PLATFORM

He has pushed the table forward. On it are the flower pot, the earth, the trowel. Astro's sleeves are rolled back in the conventional manner of magicians and he is again in full swing of a demonstration.

At start of shot, the Nubian, who has been passing among the audience with the box of mango seeds, is in the act of remounting the platform. He passes behind Astro and puts away the box and stands at attention near his master.

      ASTRO
       (continuing)
      ...And now that you have examined the earth, will the gentleman who chose the mango seed please stand up?

Astro leans over edge of platform at one side and a bearded elderly man comes into the picture and hands Astro a mango seed.

(PRODUCTION NOTE:

 These seeds are about the size of a large egg. N.W.P. is familiar with this trick having seen it in India and possessing 44 consecutive photographs of the trick taken by herself as it progressed. The detail of the performance of the trick is therefore, authentic.)

Dr. Astro accepts the seed and bows his thanks. The bearded man retires and Astro strolls back to the center of the platform as he talks, holding up the mango seed between his thumb and forefinger for the audience to see.

              (CONTINUED)

K-15 CONTINUED

                    DR. ASTRO
                    You have seen the Professor
                    Schwarts chose the seed. I
                    note that he has even marked
                    it with his name. Very good - -
                    We will now plant the seed - -
                    This is one of the most famous
                    of the Indian Fakir tricks
                    and is as childlessly simple
                    as it is ancient.

He begins the process
of planting the seed - -
putting it into the flower
pot, shoveling earth over
it, packing the earth
firmly, and finally water-
ing it with the flower
can. He then stands back
and accepts from the Nubian
a large white square of
cloth which he shows the
audience is empty. He then
throws the cloth over the
flower pot, slips his hands
under the cloth to the
flower pot, his hands being
of course, invisible, and
then begins working the
muscles of his arms without
otherwise moving.

K-14 CLOSE SHOT OF THE ABOVE

                    DR. ASTRO
                    Now, gentlemen, don't be
                    afraid to come up and watch
                    me - right up on the plat-
                    form, if you like - - that's it, - -
                    as many of you as wish to, and
                    in a few moments you will see
                    the seed sprout into a
                    tree bearing fruit. Watch
                    closely!

    DISSOLVE TO:

K-15 MEDIUM SHOT OF THE MEMBERS
     OF THE AUDIENCE . . . .

    crowding on platform
    around Astro.

    DISSOLVE TO:

NN

K-16 CRANE SHOT

    down on the closely clustered group of savants watching the trick. Dr. Astro in center at table.

    The cloth over the pot begins to rise, pushed up from below by a mass which rapidly gains in height and strength until it is about two and one-half feet tall. CAMERA is lowered to immediately above this object - - then Astro pulls away the cloth, revealing a small mango tree in full leaf, bearing golden fruit. The leaves are dripping wet and so is the fruit.

                  DR. ASTRO
           There it is, gentlemen.
           Help yourself!

    DISSOLVE TO:

K-17 THE PLATFORM

    The scientists are buzzing with interest - - examining the plant - -discussing it with each other, etc. Astro picks several of the fruit and tosses them into the audience.

    LAP DISSOLVE TO:

K-18 CLOSE SHOT OF CHARACTER COUPLE

    one of whom has caught a fruit and is astonished.

    LAP DISSOLVE TO:

NN

K-19 CLOSE SHOT OF
PROFESSOR SCHWARTZ

    and a crony to whom he is showing the seed with his name on it and the tree which has been uprooted growing from the seed.

    LAP DISSOLVE TO:

K-20 CLOSE SHOT OF JACK

    watching moodily and sulkily.

> SOUND:
> Excited murmurings of audience throughout.

    LAP DISSOLVE TO:

K-21 PLATFORM...MED SHOT

    Dr. Astro is once more alone on the platform except for the attendant Nubian. The paraphernalia of the mango trick has been removed and the Nubian is moving the two straight backed chairs to the center of the platform, placing them facing each other at a distance of four feet. Meanwhile, Dr. Astro is talking.

> DR. ASTRO
>
> Levitation, or the defiance of the laws of gravity, is another well known adjunct of magic which perhaps a few of us have ever witnessed. I will now try to show you a simple example of this art with the aid of a very charming assistant. One moment, please.

    He turns, goes to door at left, back of platform, opens it and reveals Helen.

NN
K-22 MED CLOSE SHOT
OF HELEN IN DOORWAY
FULL LENGTH PICTURE

She is clad in a very
simple evening frock of
clinging satin and is
without jewels, her whole
appearance is intentionally
simple, ladylike and quiet.
She seems in a half daze
as though she did not really
see the audience, although
she is smiling a little
fixed smile. She is already
half hypnotized.

Astro comes into the picture
takes her hand and leads
her forward. CAMERA TRUCKS
in front of them to center
of platform.

DISSOLVE TO:

K-23 CLOSE SHOT OF JACK
AND THE AUDIENCE

He recognizes Helen with a
start and half rises with
a smothered exclamation
and then sinks back.

DISSOLVE TO:

K-24 LONG SHOT OF PLATFORM
ASTRO, NUBIAN AND HELEN

Helen is lying on the chair,
her head on the back of one,
her feet on the back of the
other -- her body absolutely
rigid between them.

(PRODUCTION NOTE:
In preparing this shot,
Helen is, of course,
placed on a narrow plank
which holds her rigid, the
plank being suspended from
above on wires. She is
about 3 feet from the
floor, or the height of
the chair back.
CAMERA TRUCKS up to MED SHOT
OF THE SAME, showing Astro
standing near Helen

CONTINUED

NN K-24 CONTINUED

                                    ASTRO
                            Silence, please!

He moves toward Helen's body, makes some passes over her, moves around behind her so that his face is towards the audience behind her body. Slowly he withdraws the two chairs from under her, leaving her rigid body suspended in midair. He then holds his hands above the center of her body, but without touching it, as though he were keeping it there by magnetic suggestion emanating from his finger tips.

K-25 MED SHOT...PLATFORM...
     THE SAME...DIFFERENT ANGLE

Astro is at her head now. He goes to her, puts his hand under her head, then slides his arm along her shoulders, tipping the rigid form forward to its feet, supporting it as he does so.

K-26 CLOSE SHOT OF JACK

watching this, his face set, his fists clenched.

K-27 MED SHOT...PLATFORM
     ASTRO AND HELEN

Astro's arm is still about her. He makes some passes in front of her face with his free hand and she comes to, relaxes and stands alone, herself once more. We hear a wild outburst of the applause from the audience. Astro bows. Whemple comes into the picture at edge of platform and helps Helen off. Helen moves away into the audience.

NN

K-29 CLOSE SHOT OF HELEN

   joining Jack in audience,
   taking Jack's seat. He
   takes Whemple's vacant
   place immediately behind
   her, leans over and begins
   to question her in Whispers.

K-29 REVERSE SHOT OF WHEMPLE

   still standing just below
   the platform facing audience.

                    WHEMPLE

            Doctor Astro would like to
            know if anyone in the audience
            has another test to suggest.

   He looks about inquiring-
   ly, spots a questioner
   and signals him to speak.

            All right, over there -- what
            is it, please?

K-30 REVERSE SHOT
   A doctor has got to his
   feet.
                    DOCTOR

            Ask him if he can raise
            the dead.

   A confused murmuring
   and cries from the
   audience follow this
   remark.

K-31 REVERSE SHOT...WHEMPLE

   who nods and turns towards
   the platform.

                    WHEMPLE
                    (to Astro)

            You have heard the question,
            Dr. Astro?

K-32 REVERSE SHOT TO ASTRO

whose eyes are closed
and whose face is beginning
to look drawn and tired.

He opens his eyes suddenly
his expression alive with
interest.

K-33 CU OF DR. ASTRO'S FACE

vivid and terrible

> ASTRO
> So be it. We will indeed
> call up the dead.

K-34 FULL SHOT OF THE ROOM

The lights have been dimmed
until the audience is
hardly discernible. The
place is hushed but there
is a faint rustling now and
then. Somebody moans slightly
another laughs nervously and
then is still. The angle
is from the rear of the room
toward the platform where
Astro is seated at the table
alone, his arms folded. He
wears his cloak and one end
of it has been thrown over
his head like a cowl. His
head is slightly bowed and he
is absolutely motionless. One
shaded lamp stands on the table
beside him. At this distance
his figure suggests the
conventional pictures of
Death.

K-35 CLOSE SHOT OF HELEN AND JACK

In the darkness she has put
her head on his shoulder and
is clinging to him, frightened.
He is staring fixedly at Astro.

DISSOLVE TO:

NN

K-36 CLOSE SHOT OF ASTRO

> DR. ASTRO
> Come forth! If there be a spirit near, let him come forth!

DISSOLVE TO:

K-37 LONG SHOT OF ROOM
SAME AS BEFORE
DOUBLE EXPOSURE

On the platform, not far from Astro, appears a ghostly figure. It is a man in modern dress transparent against the background.

SOUND: Smothered screams and cries from the audience.

DISSOLVE TO:

K-38 CLOSE SHOT OF WHEMPLE
NEAR PLATFORM...

He sees the apparition and springs to his feet, gasping -- holding out his arm.

> WHEMPLE
> Joseph — my brother! Oh, God! It's Joseph!

K-39 REVERSE SHOT...PLATFORM
DOUBLE EXPOSURE...

showing phantom. The phantom is indeed the murdered Professor Whemple. The ghost turns slowly toward his living brother as if hearing him. Astro continues to sit motionless as if he, himself, were dead.

NN

K-40 CLOSE SHOT OF
JACK AND HELEN

    Jack thrusts Helen away
from him as he springs to
his feet and his arm
shoots out as he points
to the ghost.

                               JACK
                                (hoarsely)
                         Who murdered you? Speak!
                         Tell who murdered you!

K-41 MED SHOT OF PLATFORM
ASTRO AND PHANTOM
DOUBLE EXPOSURE

    At sound of Jack's voice
Astro springs to his feet
and overthrows table just
as the ghost is trying to
speak. There is a crash
the light goes out with the
overturning of the table
and there is an instant of
almost complete darkness,
full of cries, groans and
low moaning - - wailing.
Then the full lights come
on and Astro is alone on
the platform.

K-42 F.S. OF ROOM TOWARD PLATFORM

    The audience is in wild
confusion - - some of them
pushing toward the platform,
onto which Whemple has already climbed and making
his way toward Astro, who
is standing quietly there,
the Nubian behind him
protectively. We hear
exclamation of:- -

                               AD LIB

                           Marvelous!
                         Incredible!
                         I never would have believed it!
                         Wonderful

  - - etc., from the
audience

NN
K-43 CLOSE SHOT...HELEN AND JACK
oblivious of the surging
audience about her, Helen
is facing Jack in triumph
smiling. He looks dazed and
bewildered.

>   HELEN
>
>   There! Now will you believe?
>   Oh, I told you how wonderful
>   he is!

DISSOLVE TO:

K-44 EXT. OF HOUSE...ENTRANCE
MEDIUM SHOT.....NIGHT

The audience is pouring
out, finding their cars
etc.

K-45 CLOSE SHOT OF PROFESSOR
SCHWARTZ, THE FIRST
QUESTIONER AND A THIRD MAN

coming out of the house and
trying to laugh off what they
have just seen.

>   FIRST GENTLEMAN
>
>   Pure hypnotism, my dear fellow - -
>   pure hypnotism. That's all it
>   was.
>
>   PROF. SCHWARTZ
>
>   It doesn't really prove a
>   thing - - not a thing!
>
>   THIRD GENTLEMAN
>   I quite agree with you, sir
>   It was mass hypnotism - -
>   nothing more.

They come down the steps
into CAMERA

FADE OUT

-113-

SEQUENCE "L"

FADE IN:

L-1 ON FRONT DOOR OF ASTRO'S
     HOUSE ON THE PALISADES
     MEDIUM SHOT ... NIGHT

   Helen and Jack, still wearing the same clothes they
   wear at the seance, come
   into picture and Helen opens
   the door of the house with
   her key.

                    HELEN
               Good-night, Jack dear --
               Thank you for bringing me
               home.

                    JACK

               Can't I come in just for a
               moment? I hate to leave you
               alone after that horrible
               experience.

                    HELEN
               But I'm not in the least
               frightened. Well -- just
               for a moment, then.

   DISSOLVE TO:

L-2 FULL SHOT TOWER DOOR
     SHOWING ENTRANCE

   The door opens and Helen
   and Jack come in. She
   switches on the light.
   They walk down the room
   and stand near the radio-
   television machine.

L-3 CLOSE SHOT IN FRONT OF
     TELEVISION MACHINE ...
     HELEN AND JACK ...

                    JACK
               Gee, this room gives me the
               creeps. Let's have a little
               music.
                                    CONTINUED

NN
L-3 CONTINUED

>He stretches out his
>hand toward the dial but
>with a little cry Helen
>stops him.

          HELEN
>Oh, don't do that! No one
>is allowed to touch the
>radio.

          JACK
>(looking at the machine
> more carefully)
>Huh, that's funny.
>Why do you have it, then?

          HELEN
>Oh, Doctor Astro--somehow
>uses this one for experiments--
>something to do with short
>waves lengths, I think.

          JACK
>Cheerful guy, this Astro.
>Helen are you sure you are
>happy here?

          HELEN
>Well, he's wonderful to me
>of course, but . . .

>CAMERA FOLLOWS her as
>she goes over and sits
>on sofa which has an end
>table. On the end table
>is lying Max's collar
>with the charm attached.
>Jack follows and sits
>beside Helen.

          JACK
>But what?

          HELEN
>Do you sometimes--
>you'll think I'm going crazy,
>but there are things here
>that I don't like.

          JACK
>Tell me, dear.

CONTINUED

L-3 CONTINUED 2

>
> HELEN
>
> Dust! This house is full of
> dust at all the times.
> > (she leans toward him
> > and lowers her voice)
> Jack, so you know that wherever
> Doctor Astro puts his hand
> he leaves a dusty print?
>
> JACK
>
> (incredulously)
>
> What?
>
> HELEN
>
> Yes, it's so -- I swear it's
> so. I noticed it first on
> the arms of his chair, then ....
>
> JACK
>
> Yes, then?
>
> HELEN
>
> One night I woke up -- I don't
> know why -- there was no
> noise, that's sure, but there
> he was standing at the foot
> of my bed. I must have
> screamed because he went away
> at once, but on the foot of
> my bed there were two dusty
> hand prints where he had
> been leaning.

L-4 DIFFERENT ANGLE

>
> JACK
>
> Sweet, you're all shot to
> pieces. You're nervous
> tired out, imagining things,
> and this session tonight
> has been too much for you.
>
> HELEN
>
> There -- I knew you wouldn't
> believe me. And perhaps I
> did imagine it -- it's easy
> to imagine things in this
> house.
>
> JACK
>
> I wish to Heaven you'd come
> away with me now --tonight.

L-4 CONTINUED

      HELEN
    No, I can't do that. I
    must stay. Something keeps
    me here - - I hardly know
    what. But you'd better go
    now. It's getting late.

Jack sees the dog's collar lying on the little end table. He leans across Helen and picks it up.

      JACK
    Poor Max! I see you still
    treasure his collar with its
    little charm.

      HELEN
    Yes, I miss the poor darling
    dreadfully.

      JACK
      (detaching the charm
      and slipping it into
      his vest pocket)
    Do you mind if I take this
    as a souvenir?

      HELEN
    Of course not. Take it, if
    you like. That's supposed
    to be a lucky charm, you know.

      JACK
    Then perhaps it will help
    clear me regarding Whemple's
    death, and when that's done ...

He tries to take her in his arms but she repulses him, looking toward the door.

L-5 REVERSE SHOT

The door has opened and Astro in entering. He comes down the room toward them.

L-6 MED SHOT...HELEN AND JACK STANDING BY SOFA
 Astro comes into the picture and joins them.

      CONTINUED

L-6 CONTINUED

                ASTRO
                  (to Helen)
                You have guests so late,
                my dear niece?

                JACK
                I was just going. I - -

He overcomes the impulse to quarrel with Astro and turns to Helen.

                Good-night. Don't be
                nervous. Call me at any
                time and I'll come to you
                at once.

                HELEN
                Good-night

Helen and Astro watch Dr. Jack as he takes his hat and leaves.

                SOUND:
                Door closing.

Astro picks up dog's collar from sofa and holds it out to Helen.

                ASTRO
                This is yours, Iris. But,
                look - - the charm is gone!

                HELEN
                  (listlessly)
                Yes, Jack took it. He wants
                to carry it for good luck.
                Good-night.

Astro's face expresses intense satisfaction as Helen goes out of the picture. He stares in her direction even after she has gone out of the picture and laughs silently, elated at what he has heard. Then he snaps out of the mood and takes a telephone book from a nearby stand. He runs over pages and marks what he wants with a forefinger

                CONTINUED

NN

L-7 CLOSE SHOT OF
　　 TELEPHONE DIRECTORY

　　　with Astro's index finger
　　　pointing to:

　　　Foster, Dr. John, physician
　　　55 West 47th St. Cal-0624

　　　DISSOLVE TO:

L-8 TOWER ROOM...MEDIUM SHOT

　　　Astro at the city map on
　　　the wall locating this
　　　address. He crosses to
　　　television machine and
　　　begins to focus it as we - -

　　　　　　　　　　　FADE OUT

"SEQUENCE "M"

FADE IN:

M-1 ON THE METROPOLITAN MUSEUM OF ART...DAY...INT EGYPTIAN ROOM...FULL SHOT OF TOMB OF PRINCESS IRIS....

Several working men are removing the mummy of Iris from the tomb and placing it in a rough pine box on a hand truck. Dr. Astro is overseeing the task, giving directions.

M-2 MEDIUM SHOT...ASTRO, MUMMY AND WORKING MEN

ASTRO

More care there -- its very fragile.

Whemple comes into the picture

WHEMPLE

Good afternoon, Doctor What's all this?

ASTRO

The permit to remove was signed by you, Mr. Whemple. Don't you recall that I'm taking it home to my laboratory for repairs? I have better facilities and less chance of interruption up there.

WHEMPLE

Oh, yes, I remember now Ugh! It's a gruesome job but I suppose it's rather to your taste, Doctor.

DISSOLVE TO:

CONTINUED

NN

M-3 EXT. ASTRO'S HOUSE...FRONT DOOR
     MEDIUM SHOT . . . DUSK

> The working men are carrying in the mummy in its rough pine box, superintended by Astro. CAMERA FOLLOWS them into the hall where they put the mummy down inside the door. Astro pays them off. They go out of the picture and the Nubian comes in. Astro points to the coffin.

> ASTRO
> The temple -- take it there.

> The nubian lifts the lid and starts to remove the mummy.

M-4 LONG SHOT OF A STAIRWAY

> The Nubian is descending it, sharply silhouetted against the light and carrying the mummy on his back. After he has disappeared into the darkness of the cellar, (The house on the Palisades) Astro comes into the picture, also descending the stairs and silhouetted against the light. His cloak large hat and curious can all help to give him a weird bat-like appearance. Both he and the Nubian cast huge shadows on the walls as they descend.

M-5 TEMPLE...THE CELLARS
     OF THE HOUSE...FULL SHOT

> The ceiling is high, yet appears low for the length of the room which runs under the entire house. The roof is supported by squat, heavy Egyptian columns, painted and decorated with gods, symbols and scenes from the lives of the gods and from the history of Osiris, the King of the Dead.
> At the far end is the "House of the God" or shrine (see design attached)

CONTINUED

M-5 CONTINUED

In this shrine is the figure of Ammon Ra. (Design attached) The door of the shrine, a grille of iron, is closed at the moment and we do not see the god. The shrine itself, however, is embedded in the chest of a huge Sphinx figure whose head, breast and forepaws occupy the entire end of the Temple. The upper part of the giant face of the Sphinx is lost in the shadows of the ceiling, and between the enormous paws is a raised platform wide enough to accommodate twenty people standing in a row.

(Production Note: This is to accommodate the gods appearing in a later sequence)

Along the edge of this platform at intervals stand several large incense burners. Immediately below this platform is the altar, a plain oblong block, raised to a height of five feet and large enough to accommodate a human body. Close to this is a smaller block for the sacrifice of animals. This has a wooden yoke attached through which the animal's head is thrust when a sacrifice is made. The columns which support the roof run right up to the altar and on either side. The last two near the altar have curtains hanging between them, leaving a curtained off space on either side. These curtains are heavy with life-sized appliqued figures in the typical Egyptian fashion.

The end of the Temple, opposite the altar, gives the impression of being a crypt with two open tombs, in one of which rests the mummy case that Astro uses when forced to make his periodic retirement. The second tomb is empty THE CAMERA PANS from altar to crypt near which is the entrance from the stairway. The Nubian comes in carrying the mummy of Princess Iris. He is followed closely by Astro

M-6 MED SHOT...CRYPT AND
OF THE TEMPLE...

    showing coffins, Astro and
Nubian, carrying mummy case.
The Nubian sets his burden
on end against the wall in
obedience from a gesture
from Astro, then Astro points
toward the ceiling.

                    ASTRO
            The living girl - - is she at
            home?

    The Nubian nods assent.

    DISSOLVE TO:

M-7 HELEN'S ROOM M.S. EVENING

    Helen in a simple, white dress,
looking very fresh and young
is seated at her desk writing
a letter. As she chooses
stationary, takes up the pen,
adjusts light of small lamp.
etc., preparatory to writing
she is singing happily under
her breath.

M-8 CLOSE UP OF LETTER

    which reads:

    "Dear Jack"
        I have decided to take
your advise and leave this
dreadful house. I am leaving
tonight for Spring Valley and
will write you from there.

            Ever devotedly,
                Helen

M-9 MED SHOT OF HELEN AT DESK

    She hears door open - - looks
toward it.

M-10 REVERSE SHOT ... THE DOOR

    It has just closed behind Dr. Astro. He is wearing Egyptian clothing of ceremonial robe type. CAMERA PANS with him as he advances slowly until he reaches Helen and she is included in picture.

M-11 C.S. ...HELEN AND ASTRO AT DESK

    The letter is lying open on the desk between them.

> HELEN
> Oh, Dr. Astro, I'd forgotten! I'm sorry, but I can't try out an experiment tonight.
>
> ASTRO
> The hour is right - - we can not put it off.
>
> HELEN
> But - - I was going - - you said the experiment might take three days.

    Astro looks down and sees letter. He picks it up, glances at it, smiles, folds it and puts it in the envelope which is already addressed.

> ASTRO
> Ah, I see. So you wish to leave me, my dear. Well, that shall be as you wish. We will send your letter and a little later you shall go, if you still wish to do so.
>
> HELEN
> (rather shamefacedly, knowing he has read the letter)
>
> You're good - -really too good to me, but - -

CONTINUED

M-11 CONTINUED

ASTRO
(gazing deep into
her eyes - beginning to
hypnotize her)

Of course, my dear, of course.
And before you leave, you
will help me - - just the
little experiment we agreed
to try. Yes?

HELEN
(falteringly)
Yes.

ASTRO
(his face close to hers)
And you will come down with
me into the Temple of your
own free will?

HELEN
(sinking rapidly under
the hypnotic spell but
struggling under some
dimly remembered fear)

Oh, don't ask me to, please!
That dreadful place!

ASTRO
(intently)
You will consent. You are
going to obey. The soul will
depart and the soul of Iris
will take its place. Is it
not so?

HELEN
(her eyes staring
straight ahead)
It is so.

ASTRO
Then follow me - - follow - -

He moves off. Helen,
her eyes wide but sight-
less, follows.

M-12 LONG SHOT OF HELEN'S ROOM
Astro is backing away from
Helen toward the door. He
moves slowly, holding her
with his eyes. Helen is
following him at a distance
of several paces, moving
like a sleepwalker.

FADE OUT

NN

SEQUENCE "N"

FADE IN:

N-1 INT. DR JACK'S OFFICE
    MED SHOT. . . . DAY

   Dr. Jack occupies two modest
   rooms -- an office with a bedroom and bath behind it.
   He is seated at his desk.
   He takes Helen's letter from
   his pocket, opens and reads
   it.

N-2 FLASH OF LETTER
   showing it to be the same
   as Helen wrote the night
   before.

M-3 M.S. JACK AT DESK
   He picks up telephone.

                         JACK
                Hello...Long Distance, please...
                Get me Miss Helen Baratzi...
                at Spring Valley....

N-4 TEMPLE...IN THE CELLAR OF
    ASTRO'S HOUSE...FULL SHOT

   Ancient lamps have been
   lighted and placed at the
   foot of each column. Their
   flickering lights cast
   weird shadows but they illuminate
   the room sufficiently so that
   the detail is more apparent
   than during the previous shot
   of this set. ANGLE is toward
   the entrance from the stairs.
   The door is opened and through
   it come Astro and the Nubian
   leading Helen between them. She
   is clad in the simple, white dress
   in which we last saw her and
   Astro wears his robes. The
   Nubian is naked except for a
   loin cloth.

N-5 REVERSE SHOT TOWARD THE ALTAR

    The three advance toward
    the altar, CAMERA FOLLOWING
    them behind the row of
    columns at right of altar.

N-6 MED CLOSE SHOT FROM THE
ALTAR AND DIRECTLY IN FRONT
OF IT HELEN, ASTRO & NUBIAN

    She is standing between them
    still hypnotized. Astro comes
    around in front of her, his
    back to camera. He hold his
    hands a few inches from either
    side of her face so that the
    darkness of his skin is con-
    trasted against her pallor.

                              ASTRO

                    Are you ready.

    Astro's hands close over
    her face, his thumbs clos-
    ing her eyes

    DISSOLVE TO:

N-8 M.S. OF THE TEMPLE ALTAR

    Helen, in her white gown,
    is lying on the altar
    stone senseless, one hand
    hanging down helplessly over
    the edge. Astro is standing
    beside her, bending over her,
    and the Nubian kneels at this
    feet holding a tray on which
    are various lotions, small
    bottles and a hypodermic
    syringe. Astro takes this
    syringe and picking up Helen's
    hand gives her an injection
    in the arm. The Nubian
    cringes away and then looks
    up at Astro.

                              CONTINUED

nmg   N-6 CONTINUED

              NUBIAN

                  The time is short, O wise One.
                  The sands in the glass have
                  almost run again.

              ASTRO

                  What are you muttering,
                  my Shadow?

              NUBIAN

                  The hour is approaching when
                  the master must again join
                  the dead for a little while.
                  Be not betrayed by this woman
                  creature in forgetting the
                  hour, O Mighty One.

              ASTRO

                  Have no fear. My work shall
                  be swiftly done.

He watches Helen intently
for a moment, tests her
heart, makes sure she is
unconscious and moves
swiftly away, after motion-
ing the Nubian to keep
guard.

    DISSOLVE TO

N-9 STAIRS LEADING TO ABOVE
     L.S. OF ASTRO MOUNTING THEM

    DISSOLVE TO:

N-10 TOWER ROOM...FULL SHOT

    Astro enters and crosses to
    television machine.

    DISSOLVE TO:

nmg

N-11 DR. JACK'S OFFICE..MEDIUM SHOT

    Jack comes down room, switches off desk light and CAMERA FOLLOWS him into his bedroom. It is a small, simple room with a narrow single bed, bureau, etc. He turns on light, takes off his coat, which he hangs over back of chair, sits on the bed, takes off his shoes, then begins to empty his pockets, and from the vest takes several small objects, including the charm from the dog's collar.

N-12 CLOSE SHOT OF JACK'S HAND

    showing charm in it.

N-13 MEDIUM SHOT..OF JACK

    sitting on edge of bed looking at charm.

    DISSOLVE TO:

NN

N-14   TOWER ROOM
       MED SHOT OF ASTRO

   in his Egyptian robes at
   television machine busy
   focusing it.

N-15   CLOSE SHOT OF SCREEN OF
       TELEVISION MACHINE . . .

   The machine has picked up
   Jack in his bedroom, exactly
   where we left him, the charm
   in his hand.

N-16   MED SHOT OF ASTRO

   watching this. On the
   screen of television machine
   we see Jack replace the charm
   in the top pocket of his
   vest -- right over his heart.

N-17   MEDIUM SHOT IN TOWER ROOM

   Astro moves away from television machine and begins
   to trundle death ray machine
   into place, his back for a
   moment toward the screen of
   the television machine.

N-18   JACK'S BEDROOM
       MED CLOSE SHOT

   Jack gets up from his seat
   on the bed, changes his
   mind about the charm, takes
   it out of vest pocket and
   tosses it on to nearby bureau.
   Then he immediately takes
   soiled handkerchief from his
   hip pocket and throws it
   after the charm.

NN

N-19 LARGE CLOSE UP OF CHARM

    lying on top of bureau
and of the handkerchief
landing on top of it.

N-20 CLOSE SHOT OF JACK

    seated on bed again, his
head buried in his hands.

N-21 MED SHOT OF ASTRO

    with both machines focused.
He sees Jack seated on the
bed where we left him
with his head in his hands.
Jack, as seen by Astro on
screen, straightens up and
as he does so Astro lets
him have it with the death
ray.

N-22 TRICK SHOT

    The dark sky with two
zigzag lines of light
converging. This time
the shot is uneven and we
see two stars instead of
one. They burst as in
former shots of this type.

N-23 TOWER ROOM...MED SHOT

    Astro at machine sees Jack
crumple up, apparently dead.
Astro laughs.

    DISSOLVE TO:

N-24 THE LONG STAIRWAY

    leading to the Temple, showing
Astro descending hurriedly

                                           CONTINUED

NN N-24 CONTINUED
(NOTE: The wording of
the ritual used in the
following sequence is all
authentic and has been taken
from Adolph Erman's Hand book
of Egyptian Religion. This
is also true of the form of ritual.

N-25 TEMPLE...MED SHOT OF HELEN

still lying unconscious
on the sacrificial altar.
Astro comes into picture.
He looks at her, touches
her heart to make sure she
is alive, then moves away
to left of altar, THE CAMERA
PANNING with him to the
Nubian who is opening a large
basket. From this basket
the Nubian lifts a young goat,
a very pretty little live
goat with horns not yet
sprouted. The Nubian holds
the little animal while Astro
takes a small jar from a nearby stand and anoints the
head of the kid.

N-26 MED. SHOT - -

in front of the small sacrificial
block looking toward altar. The
baby goat has been fastened to
the block by the wooden yoke
ready for decapitation. The Nubian
towers above the poor little
creature, sharpening an axe.
CAMERA PANS from Nubian to the
main altar platform where Astro
is moving about lighting the
incense burners along platform's
edge.

ASTRO
(intoning as he lights
incense burners)
Praise the Thee, Osiris, son
of Hathor, who wearest the
horns and dost lean upon a
high pillar - - to whom the
crown was given and joy before
the nine gods.

He lights the last burner
and a thin spiral of
incense is rasing from each
pot. CAMERA PANS with Astro

N-26 CONTINUED

    climbs upon highest platform and faces the inner shrine. The doors of the shrine are fastened together with a cord which has seven knots in it. The cord is sealed together. Astro breaks the seal and throws the doors open revealing the God Ammon Re. As he does this, he intones:

                ASTRO
            The cord is broken and
            the seal is loosened - -
            I come. I bring thee the
            eye of Horus. Thine eye
            belongs to thee.

N-27 MED CLOSE SHOT

    Astro turns and faces camera, holds up both hands on high and cries out in a mighty voice:

                ASTRO
            Ammon Re - - the sun that is
            within the sun - - we offer
            thee blood!

N-28 REVERSE SHOT

    showing body of Helen in f.g. and beyond it the Nubian, his axe upraised. He swings it downward upon the unfortunate little goat.

N-29 MED CLOSE SHOT OF ASTRO
     AND NUBIAN

    standing near the unconscious form of Helen. In one hand the Nubian is holding the severed head of the little goat from the neck of which blood is dripping. With the other hand he holds the basin to catch this drip. Astro takes a few drops of blood as they fall and with them makes a mark on Helen's forehead and on the soles of her feet which are now bare. The Nubian   CONTINUED

NN   N-29 CONTINUED

then backs away. CAMERA
PANS with him as he disposes
of his gristly burden and
kneels by one of the columns
at a distance from the altar
but where he can watch all
that goes on. His attitude
expresses awe and fear.

N-30 FULL SHOT TEMPLE TOWARD ALTAR

The smoke from the incense
burners now arise thickly
obscuring the inner shrine.
Astro dons a long robe and
approaches altar.

N-31 MEDIUM SHOT

showing bloody block where
the goat was sacrificed,
Helen on the altar of the
main platform and shrine with
Astro conducting the mass.
The smoke of the incense
begins to fill the Temple
like a cloud.

                    ASTRO
                        (intoning)
                    My name was given me in the
                    great house and the remembrance
                    of my name in the House of
                    Flames. Hear ye, O God of
                    Egypt!

As his voice dies away
we hear the chanting of
priests (The same chant
which occurred in Scene
A-12) In the mist at the
left of the altar the chanting priests are concealed.
We see them vaguely with
indefinite forms. They appear to sway, advancing and
retreating as if they were
part of windblown mist. They
and their chant which is now
faint - - now full - -but re-
main as a background during
the rest of the sequence.

N-31 CONTINUED

    Astro turns and comes down
    from the altar.

N-32 FULL SHOT OF THE TEMPLE

    Astro strides the length
    of the Temple and takes
    up the mummy of Iris which
    has been removed from its
    case. Holding it high
    above his head he strides
    back to the altar.

N-33 REVERSE SHOT SHOWING ALTAR

    Astro walks swiftly toward
    the altar and deposits the
    mummy on the main platform.

N-34 MED SHOT OF ASTRO

    placing two ancient jars
    containing oil near the
    foot of the mummy. He then
    stands in the very center
    before the altar.

    (PRODUCTION NOTE:) Re the
    practical side of the
    remainder of the sequence:
    The following scenes are
    intended to be, pictorially
    speaking, the high spot of
    the picture. It is, there-
    fore, extremely important
    that great care and attention
    be given to its development.
    The gods who appear are ordinary
    humans wearing masks or heads
    so constructed as to resemble
    the ancient Egyptians con-
    ception of their deities. It
    is a splendid opportunity for
    using masks such as the
    Ben-da masks, with great
    effect. The idea is to present
    the apparition of the gods as
    a magnificent pageant.
    Besides the items described
    in the following scenes, there
    are many interesting creatures
    of Egyptian myology which
    could be used to great scenic
    advantage, to wit: The Vampire

CONTINUED

N-34 CONTINUED
Bat, the birds with human
heads and the serpents which
played such an important
part in all Egyptian ritual.
One interesting use is the
fact that the Sun God was
supposed to wear on his head
a blazing sun about which
writhed a live serpent.

Isis carried the full moon
between the cow's horns
which adorned her headdress.

The Bull and the Cat were
both sacred symbols in Egypt
and were mummified and buried
with great ceremony and it
would, therefore, be fitting to
use both creatures in the
processional.

In any event, the scenes which
immediately follow are only
intended as a sketchy suggestion
of the final continuity for
this particular set.)

N-35 FULL SHOT OF TEMPLE TOWARD ALTAR
Astro is working himself up
into the frenzy of the ritual.

> ASTRO
> Heed me, O Ammon Re! Take
> thou this woman's soul and
> let Iris, my beloved, enter
> in it's stead. Sun within the
> sun, hear my demand! Remember
> the gifts I have brought Thee.
> Hail Anibus, guide of the dead,
> intercede for me!

There is the sound as of
low thunder and on the altar
in the midst of the incense
Anibus, the God of Embalming,
appears before the shrine
He is half hidden between
clouds of incense which roll
around him. The singing of
the priests grow louder.
Anibus brandishes his embalming knife in token that he
has heard and moves over to
left, toward the chanting
priests and temporarily dis-
appears into the mist.

N-35 CONTINUED

Astro prostrates himself
before the apparition, then
raises himself and renews
his demands.

          ASTRO
             All ye who guide the dead
             through their dark paths
             aid thou me!

The chant of the priests
changes into a funeral
dirge as the God Wepwawet
appears. He has the head
of a jackal.

          ASTRO
             Sokaris!

The God Sokaris joins his
partner on the high plat-
form and these two guides
of the dead move slowly in
the same direction as that
taken by Anibus.

From here on the gods appear
in rapid succession. Astro
is working himself into a
frenzy. We hear the sound
of tomtoms beating as he
calls:

          ASTRO
             Sekhmet!

The lion-headed goddess of
war appears accompanied by a
retinue of Egyptian warriors
who lead slaves in chains,
captives, etc.

          SOUND:
             Screaming of slaves

They move in rhythmic
procession toward left of
the shrine.

N-36 CLOSE SHOT OF ASTRO

as he takes the two jars of
oil and pours them over the
mummy of Princess Iris and
sets fire to the oil.

N-37 LONG SHOT OF TEMPLE
     TOWARD THE ALTAR...

We have now the mounting flames added to the incense as a foreground to the entrance of the gods.

            ASTRO (intoning as he stands
                   before the altar)

         Set! Horus! O Mighty ones!
         Bast! O kind goddess, aid me!

Almost as rapidly as they are named, these deities appear. Set, the Betrayer, bent and cringing. Bast is the cat goddess, a goddess of plenty, and she is accompanied by a retinue of field toilers, sheaves and grain, garlands of grapes. Horus is the all-seeing god who guards the eyes of the world. (A good trick shot might be made, with double exposure, of detached human eyes, enormous in size, with Horus a figure of normal height passing among them)

            ASTRO
              Isis! I invoke Thee, the
              great mother goddess!

Isis appears. She is distinguished by her curious headdress and her hawk wings.

N-38 CLOSE SHOT OF NUBIAN

Kneeling by the column, his eyes staring, his head swaying as if he were seeing all this in a hypnotic dream.

N-39 MED SHOT TOWARD ALTAR

            ASTRO
              Hathor! Goddess of love,
              aid me in this hour!

                   CONTINUED

-138-

NN
N-39 CONTINUED

    The chant of the priests turns to light, staccato music. We hear the clashing of cymbals and the tinkle of the little cup used by oriental dancing girls. The dance rhythm becomes more pronounced, and at first singly, then in groups, the dancing girls of the goddess of love begin to appear, heralding her approach. They are black almost nude, with small square aprons and sharply outlined head-dresses. They whirl into view, half hidden in the mist, dancing - - posturing - - turning to bow before the advance of the goddess, then whirl about again. They are followed by a group of boys bearing heavy garlands of flowers. The boys laugh, sing, chase the girls - - and on their heels comes the goddess of love herself, reclining on a couch which is set upon a barge-shaped vehicle, drawn by two white oxen who are guided by elaborately costumed slaves. On her head she wears the moon and the stars gleam in her robes.

    Astro prostrates himself before the vision as it passes, and then gathering his strength for a last tremendous effort, he staggers nearer to the inner shrine.

                    ASTRO
            Ammon Re! The sun that is
            within the sun!

N-40 CLOSE SHOT OF THE SHRINE

    The doors are open showing Ammon Re in effigy, double exposure. The figure stirs and comes to life, starts to step forth. (See production note Scene N-34

NN

N-41 LONG SHOT OF TEMPLE
      TOWARDS ALTAR...

   The mummy has been consumed and nothing remains of it but a heap of ashes. The whole procession of gods weaves back and forth around the prostrate figure of Astro and the unconscious form of Iris, the scene being dominated by the Sun God, Ammon Re.

N-42 CLOSE SHOT OF NUBIAN

   who has fallen flat on his face and is groveling in abject fear. The Nubian then raises himself slowly and a bewildered look comes over his face.

N-43 FULL SHOT OF TEMPLE
      TOWARDS ALTAR....

   The lights are dim and the gods are gone.

N-44 MED SHOT OF THE TEMPLE
      TOWARDS ALTAR.....

   showing Helen. Astro still prostrated before the shrine. He gets up slowly and moves toward Helen who is staring at him. He reaches her and bends over her. She raises both her arms and puts them around his neck.

N-45 CLOSE SHOT..HELEN AND ASTRO

   She smiles up at him and raises herself. His arms go about her. Their attitude is that of accustomed lovers.

                              CONTINUED

N-45 CONTINUED

                  HELEN
                    (smiling at him)

                Beloved! I had such a
                strange dream. I thought
                that I had died.

                  ASTRO
                    (tenderly)

                Iris! Iris! at last!
                Now, you shall never die!

                  HELEN

                It was as though my soul
                had gone from me.
                (she clutches him to her)
                Don't let me dream such
                dreams again!

                  ASTRO

                Iris, say that you love me.
                Say that you will never leave
                me.

                  HELEN

                I love you.

He buries his face in
her shoulder as we --

DISSOLVE TO:

N-46 DR. JACK'S BEDROOM F.S.

Jack's body is lying across
the bed as we left it.
Dawn is showing through
window. CAMERA TRUCKS up
to CLOSE SHOT OF JACK'S
BODY. He stirs and moans,
lifts one hand waveringly
as he feels for an injury.
Then he begins to rise slowly,
still sick from the shock,
but with rapidly returning
consciousness.

N-46 CONTINUED

>He gets up slowly and painfully. CAMERA TRUCKS BACK to MEDIUM SHOT of same. Jack is on his feet now, swaying slightly, dazed and trying to decide what happened to him. He sniffs the air -- something has been burning and the atmosphere of the room is stifling. He looks about and his eye lights on the handkerchief he had thrown on the bureau. It is scorched almost to a cinder. He strides across to it and picks it up.

N-47 CLOSE SHOT OF SCORCHED HANDKERCHIEF.....

>Jack's hand picks it up revealing the "lucky" charm which he had removed from the dog's collar. The bureau directly under the charm is charred. Jack's other hand picks up the charm revealing a star-like burn similar to the burn found on the dead dog, and earlier, on the breast of Professor Whemple.

N-48 MED CLOSE SHOT OF JACK

>examining the charm and charred spot on the bureau.

>>JACK
>>First the Professor --
>>then the dog -- and now --

>he breaks the charm open.

N-49 C.S. OF BROKEN CHARM

>Inside is a small wire coil with an electrical contact spot in the center.

N-50 MED CLOSE SHOT

    Jack looking at the broken
    charm in horror, realizing
    his narrow escape from death.
    He then pulls himself to-
    gether, realizes he must get
    action, throws on his coat,
    grabs his hat, tucks charm into
    pocket and rushes for the door.

    DISSOLVE TO:

N-51 TEMPLE...MED SHOT TOWARD ALTAR

    Astro is assisting Helen down
    from the altar block, puts his
    arm about her waist and she
    lets her head fall back on his
    shoulder as with every evidence
    of affection they walk toward
    the great curtains hanging be-
    tween the two columns immediately
    at right of altar. CAMERA
    FOLLOWS them to where the Nubian
    stands holding one of the cur-
    tains back and continues to
    follow them through into small
    recess furnished like a roam in
    early Egyptian style. It is a
    boudoir such as might have be-
    longed to an Egyptian princess.
    There is a couch, a stand with
    perfumes, a small table on which
    are laid out the jewels of the
    Princess Iris from the museum,
    and a hand-mirror. The room is
    bedecked with lotus flowers in tall
    vases and lighted softly by
    antique lamps.

    Astro and Helen seat themselves
    on the couch.

N-52 DIFFERENT ANGLE ON COUCH

    showing that the Nubian has
    let the curtain fall behind
    them, leaving himself outside
    in Temple.

                   HELEN
          Tell me, Beloved, what Temple
          is this, or what Palace - -
          I cannot seem to remember.

                                          CONTINUED

N-52 CONTINUED

          ASTRO
           (tenderly)

          Iris, my love, you have been asleep for a long, long time. Be not afraid when I tell you that you are in a strange land.

          HELEN

          I am not afraid -- with you! But it seems as though I had lost you -- as though you had been taken from me.

          ASTRO

          For three thousand years!

          HELEN

          An hour is a thousand years when you are gone.

She leans toward him and they kiss.

N-53 C.S...ASTRO AND HELEN

    As they embrace and kiss

N-54 MED CLOSE SHOT OF THE TWO

    on the couch embraced. They draw apart and Helen sees the jewels on the small table close to the couch. She leans over and picks up the necklace.

          HELEN

          My jewels! Oh, beloved, I would make myself more beautiful for thou.

She puts on the necklace

          ASTRO

          Bedeck thyself, Iris, for this is thy wedding night.

Helen has picked up the mirror and started to preen herself before her reflection in it. She looks at him startled

CONTINUED

NN
N-54 CONTINUED

      HELEN
     Our wedding night?

      ASTRO
     Have we not waited long
     enough?

      HELEN
     Thou art right. It has been
     too long.

He draws her back into his arms unresisting. They sink back on the couch together. Astro's hand slips from her head to her shoulder and the white satin of her dress. As he leans over he sees his hand, lifts it and notes with horror that it has left a dusty imprint on her gown.

      ASTRO
     Too long!

Suddenly horrified at what he as seen, he pushes her from him and arises.

     Iris, do you know -- can
     you guess how long I have
     waited?

      HELEN
     A day -- a week -- a moon,
     perhaps?

      ASTRO
     It is true when I tell thee
     it has been three thousand
     years.

      HELEN
     Why dost thou jest?

      ASTRO
     It is no jest but truth --
     Look you, I have found the
     secret of eternal life --
     of how to keep my limbs
     together, the brain within
     my skull where should be
     only dust and barren bone.

NN   N-55 DIFFERENT ANGLE

Helen has got up from the
couch and is backing away
from him, still, however,
not taking him quite
seriously.

                      HELEN
                          Then, how am I so young
                          and fresh?

                      ASTRO
                          You were, an hour since
                          a mummy in a tomb - -but
                          by my magic I have given
                          you good flesh; flesh so
                          white and sweet - - so
                          gracious to me - - soon!

He laughs hysterically
and comes toward her with
outstretched arms as we

DISSOLVE TO:

N-56 INT. OF WHEMPLE'S HOUSE
      LIVING ROOM...DAY
      MEDIUM SHOT........

Whemple and Jack before
fireplace. Jack has his
hat on the back of his
head. He shows signs of
great excitement. In his
hand is the broken charm
which he is showing to
Whemple.

                    JACK
                        (continuing)
                        - - And it explains your
                        brother's murder perfectly.

                  WHEMPLE
                        This coil attracted the death
                        ray, without a doubt!

                  JACK
                        (frantically)
                        But we must act! Act!
                        That fiend may have her
                        there alone, and God knows...
                  WHEMPLE
                        We'd better get help from the
                        police - - it may be necessary
                        to break in. Come with me.

Both men move hurriedly
towards the door.   DISSOLVE TO:

N-57 LITTLE CHAMBER OFF TEMPLE

Same shot as N-55, with Helen and Astro in same position, he laughing hysterically and coming toward her with outstretched arms.

> ASTRO
> Come with me and I will prove my words.
>
> HELEN
> It seems so strange.
>
> ASTRO
> Come!

He takes her by the hand and leads her toward curtain which cuts off Temple.

DISSOLVE TO:

N-58 TEMPLE...MED SHOT SHOWING CRYPT AND THE TWO TOMBS...

Helen and Astro come into the picture, he leading her. They stop before the tombs.

> ASTRO
> (continuing)
>
> --And here, beloved Iris, is my resting place. Once every three moons I must be as the dead in order that the fine oils and secret essences known to the ancient priests may do their work. In my shroudings I must lie until new strength is sucked into my dry and brittle flesh. Then, I come forth again to live anew.
>
> HELEN
> (awed)
> And so you live forever?
>
> ASTRO
> And so I live forever.
>
> HELEN
> What is that place beside then?

CONTINUED

-147-

N-58 CONTINUED

        ASTRO
    That is thy place.

        HELEN
    My place? No- - no! Cease
    they jest, lover of mine.

        ASTRO
      (grimly)
    I do not jest. The time
    grows short and soon I must
    go down to the dead.

        HELEN
    And how long must thou remain
    in the underworld, Osiris?

        ASTRO
    Twelve days.

        HELEN
      (still incredulous)
    Twelve days! And must I wait
    so long for thee?

        ASTRO
    No - - this time thou shall
    come with me!

He sways slightly as
though feeling a sudden
weakness.

    Thou shall come with me.
    Iris

He raises his hand, shakes
it at her half playfully,
and to his horror and hers
a peppering of dust falls
from his fingers. Helen
backs away.

N-59 C.S. HELEN AND ASTRO

        HELEN
      (recoiling)
    No! No! I want no traffic
    with the dead!
        ASTRO
    Iris! Hear me. You shall
    be made even as I - - a
    mummified thing that yet
    lives.

CONTINUED

N-59 CONTINUED

      HELEN

       No - - I tell thee! No!
       I love this beautiful young
       body too well, I will not
       die again!

      ASTRO
       But you shall die only to
       live forever through all the
       ages.

He brings his face close
to hers and tries to
strengthen his hypnotic
hold on her, but his powers
are failing him.

       Iris, you will obey!

Helen looks at him with
growing terror as the
hypnotic spell under which
she has been, starts to
diminishing strength

      HELEN
       I will not die! I will not!

She turns and runs from
him.

DISSOLVE TO:

N-60 TEMPLE...F.S. TOWARD ALTAR

Helen is running toward the
altar and Astro is pursuing
her, but his strength is
failing him rapidly and as he
moves dust falls from his
clothing. Helen reaches
the altar, looks frantically
from the curtains on the
right to the curtains on the
left, hesitates, decides it
is the left side she is search-
ing for and dashes to the
curtains, starting to pull
them back just as Astro all
but reaches her.

-149-

NN   N-61 MED CLOSE SHOT
OF HELEN AT CURTAINS
She pulls them back revealing the Nubian. He is standing beside a slab-like table
over which water is running - -
This table is of stone, not
quite horizontal, and bears
on its upper surface a faint
indentation the size and
shape of a human body; it is
in fact, the replica of an
ancient Egyptian embalming
table. Beside this on a stand
are the knives incenses
needles, coarse thread, bandage
rolls, etc., - - all the equipment for embalming as practised
by the Egyptians.

The Nubian stands bot upright
waiting ominously. Helen
screams and turns about only
to face Astro standing directly
behind her. His face has grown
ashen and terrible.

                ASTRO
          Ha! Ha! See - - we are
          well prepared for you!
                HELEN
          You monstrosity! Don't
          touch me!
                ASTRO
          Iris - - obey! It is our
          last chance for eternity
          together.
                HELEN
          I cannot do it! I will not
          submit!
                ASTRO
          (thickly)
          You must!

Helen cowers back against
the curtain as Astro makes
a feeble hypnotic pass at
her with both terrible hands
from which the dust falls
thickly. He then perceives
that he can no longer influence
her and that she is rapidly
regaining her senses.
Furiously, Astro turns to the
Nubian.

                ASTRO
          Come hither, slave!

N-62 M.S....ASTRO, HELEN, NUBIAN

The Nubian advances, a huge naked knife in his hand.

      ASTRO
    Take the woman! Embalm her --
    make haste so that she may
    go with me. The time is
    very short.

The Nubian, accustomed to obeying, strides toward Helen who shrieks and crouches further into the billowing curtains.

DISSOLVE TO:

N-63 CITY STREET...LONG SHOT

with police car tearing through the traffic.

      SOUND:
    Helen's shriek is taken
    up by the sirens of the
    police car going full
    blast.

DISSOLVE TO:

N-64 THE TEMPLE...MEDIUM SHOT

The Nubian is still advancing on Helen. As he reaches her and towers over her with knife raised above his head, he hesitates, drops the knife and faces Astro.

N-65 REVERSE SHOT

Astro sees this and curses the Nubian.

      ASTRO
    You, too! May the curse
    of Amen rest upon you!

NN   N-66 CLOSE UP OF NUBIAN

                    NUBIAN

                    The woman shall live!

DISSOLVE TO:

N-67 EXT. ASTRO'S HOUSE
      FRONT DOOR...MED SHOT

   Police, Dr. Jack and Whemple
   are battering at the door
   demanding admission.

                    AD LIB
                       Answer!

                    Open up!

                    In the name of the law! etc.

DISSOLVE TO:

N-68 THE TEMPLE...MED SHOT
      GROUP BESIDE CURTAINS
      HELEN, ASTRO AND NUBIAN

                    JACK'S VOICE
                       (calling)
                       Helen! Helen! Where are
                       you, Helen?

   Helen hears, and the sound
   of Jack's voice breaks the
   last shred of Astro's spell
   over her. She straightens
   up from her crouching position
   and attempts to escape, but
   Astro seizes and holds her.

                    HELEN
                       Jack! Jack!

                    ASTRO
                       Help me, O Hathor! Help me,
                       Gods of Egypt!
                    HELEN
                       (to Nubian)
                       Let them in! Let them in!
                       Go!

                    CONTINUED

-152-

NN
N-68 CONTINUED

   The Nubian starts to
   obey. Astro sees this
   and in his excitement almost
   lets go of Helen.

                    ASTRO
                       (to Nubian)
                    Hold the door, slave!
                    Let no one pass!
                    HELEN
                       (to Nubian)
                    Go, my friend -- please
                    Help me!

   DISSOLVE TO:

N-69 TEMPLE...FULL SHOT
      SHOWING EXIT TO STAIRS

   Helen and Astro are struggling in the middle of the
   floor. The Nubian tuns towards exit, flings open the
   door to stairs and dis-
   appears.

                    SOUNDS:
                    Pounding and knocking
                    from above and a police
                    whistle blowing.

   Now begins a chase of
   Helen by Astro. She breaks
   away and he, though growing constantly more feeble,
   goes after her and almost
   gets her again. She eludes
   him but he manages to keep
   between her and the exit
   to the stairs until, with
   a sudden twist, she dashes
   around him barely escaping
   his clutching hands and makes
   a bolt for freedom. She all
   but reaches the door when
   panting and exhausted, she
   falls in a faint on the floor.
   Astro wavers toward her for
   a second and then turns away.

N-70 CLOSE SHOT OF ASTRO

   His face has begun to decay
   and his eyes are gone. He
   is blind

   DISSOLVE TO:

NN   N-71 TEMPLE...FULL SHOT
           TOWARD ALTAR....

   Astro, thinking himself
   quite alone, his strength
   all but gone, staggers
   toward the altar and stands
   before it swaying, his arms
   uplifted.

N-72 MED SHOT OF SAME

   Astro before the altar
   his back to CAMERA, his
   arms upraised in sup-
   plication.

                    ASTRO
                         (making dreadful, in-
                         articulate sounds)

           DISSOLVE TO:

N-73 ENTRANCE HALL...UPSTAIRS
     SHOWING FRONT DOOR...
     MEDIUM SHOT........

   The Nubian, panting, drip-
   ing with sweat, is in the
   act of opening the door.
   As it opens, Jack, Whemple,
   Police Commissioner Jennings
   and some uniformed police
   burst into the hall.

                    JACK

                         Where is she?

                    WHEMPLE

                         Take us to your master,
                         you brute!

                    JENNINGS & POLICE
                         (Ad lib)
                         Better watch out!
                         Draw your guns, boys!
                         Careful there!
                         No tricks now, etc.

   Nubian leads way
   to stair head.

NN

N-74 L.S. WINDING STAIRS

   leading down to Temple
   with Whemple. Commissioner,
   police, etc. following
   Nubian down, and led by
   Jack.

   DISSOLVE TO:

N-75 L.S TOWARDS DOOR TO STAIRS

   The crumpled white heap
   which is Helen's unconscious
   figure, is barely discernible
   in middle background. The
   group, which has descended
   the stairs, crowds into the
   Temple and then stops dead
   at the entrance, paralysed
   with horror by what they are
   seeing.

N-76 REVERSE SHOT, MED CLOSE
     UP TOWARD ALTAR ...

   Astro hears their entrance
   and wheels about to face
   them, and before our eyes
   we see the horror which has
   halted the intruders, for
   we watch Astro decay by the
   same method of stop shots
   which was used in Dr. Jekyll
   and Mr. Hyde. He rots away
   before our gaze, shrinks and
   crumples to a dusty shell
   which collapses in a heap
   on the floor before the
   altar.

                              SOUND:
                                 Voice of the Nubian
                                 giving a great cry.

N-77 FULL SHOT TOWARDS ALTAR

   The Nubian springs away
   from the officers who are
   holding him, rushes forward
   and falls dead on the remains of his master.

   DISSOLVE TO:

NN   N-78 MED SHOT OF JACK

    picking up the prostrate
    form of Helen.

                    JACK

              Helen, darling! Helen!

    She opens her eyes
    and stirs

N-79 C.U. HELEN AND JACK

    as he clasps her to him.

                  FADE OUT

                  THE END